Prince Charming *is* Dead... *or in* Rehab!

A Guide to Dating in the Real World

Janice Sterling Gaunt

Foreword by Tova Sido - Author of *Borrowed Courage*

outskirts
press

*I joyfully dedicate this book to my three
fabulous daughters, Brynn, Wesley, and Blair; my nine
totally amazing grandchildren, Skylar, Charlie Mae, Wyatt,
Huxley, Harlowe, Truett, Owen, Haney, and Mia; and
my kind and unbelievably supportive husband, Tom.
All of you are the freaking bomb!!!*

Table of Contents

Foreword

In 2014, my marriage went from complete bliss to, well, total shit. Overnight. I had been married fifteen years, and the bomb that went off in my home was something I never thought I would have to go through. Never wanted to experience. I did the one thing people often do when their marriage is in trouble; I called my best friend. My best friend suggested I make an appointment with her therapist, Janice Gaunt. In my first phone call to Janice, I couldn't even speak I was crying so hard. Walking into Janice's office was one of the best decisions I have ever made in my life. Over the next several years, Janice worked (very patiently, I'll add) to help me navigate the fantasy of my blissful marriage, through my divorce, dating, to my now engagement and combining two families. This work is not for the faint of heart. I had no idea how to walk away from my marriage and the man I had loved since I was fourteen years old. I had no idea how to tell my children and be a single mom. I sure as hell had no idea how to date! I had not been on one of those in decades! Navigating these last few years has been some of the darkest and most difficult times of my life, and let me tell you something: I stubbed my toe, again and again and again. Getting divorced and starting to date again made me feel like a complete idiot. And that's all *with* Janice's wisdom and expertise! I can't imagine how I would have ever been able to get to the other side without her. If someone told me in 2014 that over the next several years I would regain my life, my finances, and my self-worth, I would have never believed them. But here I am, living proof that with the right kind of help and support system, we can all get through anything.

Prince Charming Is Dead...Or in Rehab! is nothing short of BRILLIANT! I feel like the years of therapy is summed up perfectly in these ten chapters. This book is overflowing with so many great examples, inspiring wisdom, and sound advice. It includes everything from dating, sex, combining families, how to communicate, have productive conflict, and my personal favorite, how to take good care of yourself through it all. Every single one of these chapters is practical and so incredibly helpful. When I read through the chapters I can hear Janice's voice—just as if I were sitting in her office. The only thing missing is I don't get to see her fabulous choice in shoes! I love how Janice is the perfect balance of wisdom, grace, and...self-deprecation. Half the reason she shares such sound wisdom is from all that she has personally gone through herself. That experience is invaluable and allows the reader to trust her insight. Plus, she has a wicked sense of humor and at times a little irreverent (one of my favorite qualities in any human).

If you are a person who is interested in experiencing the best in your romantic relationships (who doesn't want this??) all the while staying true to yourself in the process, this book is for you! *Prince Charming Is Dead...Or in Rehab!* will leave you feeling empowered and infuse you with much-needed tools for your dating (and married) life. Get out your highlighter, and get ready to dog-ear some pages. This will sit on your bedside so you can pick it up again and again!

To your healthiest and happiest life and love,

Tova Sido

Acknowledgments

Without great mentors, it would have been impossible for me to write this book and to do what I do with my clients. In 1999, I attended a Post Induction training workshop at The Meadows Treatment Center in Wickenburg, Arizona. It was there that Pia Mellody first introduced me to the concept of toxic shame. Pia taught me how the lack of nurturing love creates a wound within a child that affects the child throughout his life, and the importance of healing those childhood wounds. My training with Terrence Real, founder of the Relational Life Institute in Boston, Massachusetts, brought me into an even deeper understanding of toxic shame and grandiosity. Terry trained me to recognize the effects of toxic shame in relationships and to guide my clients on a path of relationship repair. Thank you, Pia and Terry, for your genius, your inspirational work, and for your generosity in sharing with me your wisdom and truth.

To all of the women, men, and adolescents with whom I have worked, thank you! I greatly admire your courage, tenacity, and willingness to learn and change. As your teacher, I have been your student.

I also want to acknowledge my besties, Kathryn Cook, Julie Crenshaw, Pam Dyer, Mary Clare Finney, Blair Knouse, and Vicki Saviers. You have been my salvation during the difficult times, my sources of great fun during the good times, and my encouragers through graduate school and my writing endeavors. I humbly thank you with all of my being.

Thank you, Tom, for believing in this project from the beginning. As a loving husband and friend, I cannot imagine anyone being more supportive. I also want to thank my daughters Brynn, Wesley, and Blair for cheering me along in my desire to make the world a better place.

Thank you Sadie V. and everyone at Outskirts Press for believing in me and providing me with the wisdom and resources to implement my vision.

Preface

In 1995, I began one of the most painful journeys of my life. After twenty-two years of marriage, I realized that I was headed for divorce. At the time, I could not even say the "D" word without feeling great despair and sadness. I believed I was an absolute failure and terribly fearful that my three precious daughters would be eternally messed up. I remember sobbing uncontrollably in the fetal position on my closet floor as my daughters stood by and helplessly watched. I was a hot mess!

Because I had no sense of self away from my marriage, I did not think I could survive. Life as I knew it was ending, and I literally wanted to die.

Fortunately, I sought professional help and was able to begin again. My therapist educated me about shame and guided me down the pathway to healing. Because I grew to understand the affects that shame had on my ability to make sound life decisions, it was necessary for me to fix my "picker"—that is, how I approached the choosing of romantic partners. I did not want to repeat the same experience in some alternate form.

As I began to heal from my shame, I started to believe I deserved abundance in all areas of my life. I also thought that perhaps I could use my pain to help others with theirs, therefore making mine purposeful. This revelation inspired me to attend graduate school. After four years of hard work and perseverance, I earned my master's degree in counseling and became a licensed professional counselor.

For over twenty years, I've counseled both men and women of all ages, and I know I've been doing exactly what I'm supposed to do with my life. I also realize that all my experiences were necessary so that I could first heal myself and then in some small way contribute to the healing of others.

A year into graduate school, I decided that it was time to get out there and try dating. I was a grown woman of forty-four years feeling like a naïve girl of sixteen who knew nothing about how to date. I jumped into the dating world with both feet just to see what might happen.

I went out with some great guys and some awful guys. I was wined and dined, dumped, and proposed to. There were a couple of wealthy men with private jets (which I have to admit was a lot of fun), a guy with horrific road rage, one who had been married three times (I would have been *Señora*

Cuatro), and a few men so narcissistic that any time I started talking about me and my life, they would change the subject back to themselves. I "fell in love" way too early with a couple of these guys without giving them enough time to show me who they really were. As a result of my naïveté about dating and my fantasy about Prince Charming coming to the rescue, I ignored some obvious warning signs, and my heart took a beating.

I decided to bid adieu to the parade of Mr. Wrongs and give the dating game a rest.

Several months later, my middle daughter came home from a yoga class and told me something astonishing: she and her sister had given my name and phone number to a random guy named Tom who was in their class! It was their idea! She told me they stopped him as he left the class, handed him my information, and said, "We think you should take out our mom. You guys have the same energy."

Thinking that they meant an elderly gentleman named Tom who I knew attended the yoga class, I responded with, "Are you crazy? You gave Grandpa my number?"

"No," she replied. "We gave your number to the *younger* guy named Tom."

Oh. I had a vague awareness of Young Tom. I was absolutely mortified! I did not think for a minute that he would call unless he happened to be a desperate loser. I put him out of my mind.

Three days later, Tom called. I was shocked, but to be polite and to satisfy my busybody matchmaking daughters, I agreed to meet him one morning at Starbucks for coffee. Or in Tom's case, as I found out, not coffee, only tea.

To my amazement, I discovered that my daughters were quite right.

On our one-year dating anniversary, Tom suggested that we relive our first date at the same Starbucks where we met. After sipping tea and coffee for a few minutes, he asked me to marry him! My daughters had done a much better job of picking a great guy for me than I had done in my ten years of post-divorce dating.

We're still happily married, and he's definitely my Mr. Marvelous!

Through my own dating experiences, and having had the great fortune of being trained by two whom I consider to be the best therapists in existence, Pia Mellody and Terrence Real, I discovered there are many dating issues and principles that are applicable no matter what one's age. People simply do not know how to date effectively in the real world. When talking about this revelation and explaining the dating skills with my clients, friends, and family members, people kept telling me that I should write a dating book. This idea rambled around in my brain for about fifteen years until I decided to give it a go. *Prince Charming Is Dead...Or in Rehab!* is the culmination of these skills and practices.

Thank you for inviting me to share my knowledge with you. I feel excited and privileged to walk with you through your dating experiences and help you find Mr. Marvelous. Enjoy!

Introduction:
You've Come a Long
Way, Baby

"I've been on so many blind dates,
I should get a free dog."
—Wendy Liebman

Well, well, well...here you are, contemplating a brave entry into the potentially perilous arena of dating. Although this could be your first go at the dating scene, chances are, it is not. Due to their naïve understanding about finding a partner, most first-timers do not read self-help books on dating. They have been neither the *dumpee* nor the *dumper*, so they do not realize that the dating game is often complicated and emotionally painful.

There are a few who actually enjoy the dating process, but most people date simply as a means to an end. They approach dating as a crapshoot: they roll the dice by going on a date, and if they roll a 7 or 11, they are a winner! Even though there is an element of chance in the way people meet, I am going to introduce you to some very specific skills that will teach you how to date effectively. These skills will optimize your chances of meeting Mr. Marvelous as well as making the dating process much more predictable and enjoyable.

Along with teaching you these skills, my goal is to move you from *needing* a relationship to *wanting* a relationship. I want to show you how to play the dating game differently and to encourage you to take care of your body, mind, and spirit because it's good for you, not because it is a seduction tool! As I guide you through the three stages of dating—Dating Bootcamp (preparing to date), The Dating Game (the dos and don'ts of how to play the game), and I Think This Is My "Boo" (from wedding to keeping the fire alive)—you'll gain a feeling of empowerment and self-esteem. *Prince Charming Is Dead...Or in Rehab!* invites you to open your mind to learning a new way of thinking about the dating process and to make it fun and stress-free.

Section I:

Dating Boot Camp

Sarah

"Sometimes it takes a heartbreak to shake us awake
and help us see we are worth so much
more than we're settling for."
—Mandy Hale

Sarah, a beautiful and brilliant young attorney, had been a client of mine for several years. At age forty-four, her endless romantic struggle centered around her on-again, off-again boyfriend, a handsome and successful investment banker named David. Ten years her senior, he was very generous and adoring toward her when it was convenient and easy for him. But if he was overwhelmed at work or focused on helping his aging parents, Sarah was the first thing to go. I mean in a big way: the guy would simply ignore her messages and calls. Total radio silence.

Each and every time he broke off contact, Sarah was heartbroken and swore up and down that she was committed to never date the rat again. But after a few weeks of not finding another man who floated her boat, Sarah would pick up the phone and call David. He would eventually respond and weasel his way back into her life.

One day, having not seen Sarah for over a year, I was shocked at her appearance when she entered my office. As befitting her profession, Sarah's manner of dress was typically the epitome of high fashion along with the latest haircut, designer shoes, and an enviable handbag. But on this particular day, Sarah was dressed in sweatpants and a ripped T-shirt, like she had put them on to clean her bathroom. Her uncombed hair hung in her face as she flopped down on my couch and broke into tears.

"Please tell me what's been happening with you," I said.

"It happened again," she sobbed. "David and I had been dating for about four months, and everything seemed to be perfect! I mean we had our occasional arguments but nothing too big. As usual, our sex life was amazing, and if I did not mention marriage or moving in together, David treated me like a queen. Last week, David's mother was diagnosed with a benign breast tumor. Fortunately, it's very treatable. But as soon as David got the news, he became unreachable. It's like he he's fallen off the face of the earth. What is wrong with me?"

"Sarah," I began gently, "The only thing that is wrong with you is that you keep going back to him knowing that he has done this to you before. His disappearing act has nothing to do with you. It affects the heck out of you and your life, but it truly is not about you. He's simply unavailable because of his enmeshment with his parents and his perception that it is his duty to prioritize his work and parents over you. Because David does not have the emotional maturity to create a healthy balance in these areas, he gets overwhelmed and runs for the hills. I've seen his type before. He's Mr. Dance Away."

"But why am I the one left out in the cold?" Sarah cried. "Doesn't he love me? Am I not good enough? I try to give him everything he wants." After a pause she added, "I'm so scared to be alone."

"Honestly, Sarah," I replied, "it's not you— he would do the same to any woman. It's not about David not loving you or that you're not skinny enough, sexy enough, pretty enough, or understanding enough. You are not supposed to be needless and wantless in a relationship, and until David does some extensive family of origin work, this pattern will not change."

She nodded and dabbed her eyes with a tissue. Her breathing slowed, and her face began to relax.

"By the way," I said, "you and I need to revisit and strengthen some of your self-care skills. Your familial fear of abandonment issues have been triggered again, so it's essential for us deal with those. Once you take care of that scared little girl living inside of you, you'll feel empowered enough to get off this merry-go-round. You deserve so much better!"

"I know," Sarah said as she took a deep breath. "I simply cannot ever do this again. Let's schedule another appointment."

Chapter 1
Clean Out the Closet

You may have once found yourself in Sarah's shoes, pining for Disappearing David, who had proven, over and over again, that he was unavailable.

Sarah had a deep-rooted fear of being abandoned. And so what man did she choose? A man who periodically abandoned her, thus fulfilling her fear.

Ladies, we do this to ourselves more often than we'd care to admit!

Let's get back to basics.

Before you start looking for Mr. Marvelous, I'm sure you have a closet full of ineffective dating skills that need to be addressed along with some emotional housekeeping from past failed relationships. Doing the same thing over again and expecting a different result is not only insanity but exhausting and discouraging. Your time is valuable and your heart is fragile, so learning how to spend some nurturing time with yourself will be time well spent.

Let's clean out your relationship closet and get you empowered!

Here are the steps you should take:

Grieve the Loss of the Previous Relationship

If it's been less than six months since your last serious relationship ended, you need some more time to grieve that loss. I believe that it takes from six months to a year to effectively grieve the loss of any relationship, especially if the last relationship lasted more than a few months. You must have hung around for that long because you wholeheartedly believed that this guy had the potential of being Mr. Marvelous. As another one bites the dust, it is important that you understand and lean into the grief.

The grieving process has five stages: denial, anger, bargaining, depression (sadness), and acceptance. People do not necessarily go through the stages in order. Instead, they dance around the stages until they settle in the fifth stage, acceptance. The acceptance stage does not mean that you are necessarily okay with the way things happened. It means that it is what it is, and you're ready to go on with your life without the sadness, shame, or anger. The feelings experienced with the other stages must be felt and allowed to dissipate with time. These feelings are typically sadness, fear, anger, guilt, and shame. Feeling these feelings is like withdrawing from a drug. As you withdraw from the relationship high you experienced during the good parts of the relationship, the pain is real. Even though the feelings are usually uncomfortable, they will not kill you. I promise! One of my favorite sayings is, "Rejection is God's protection." As I look back on my dating history, this saying has proven to be true. There is not one past relationship that I regret not working.

Even if it was your idea to end the relationship, you still need to go through the grieving process. After all, you dated this person for a reason, so there will be some parts of the relationship that you will miss.

In my own case, during and after my divorce, I had no capacity to identify and verbalize what I was feeling. One day I was in a group therapy session and tears started streaming down my face. The therapist asked me what I was feeling.

I blubbered, "I don't know what I'm feeling!"

She pointed to a chart on the wall, which conveniently identified the eight basic feelings.

When I saw the word "sadness," I said, "I guess I feel sad." Because I grew up in a family system that did not talk about feelings, I'm not sure I had ever said the words "I feel sad." Rather than being vulnerable and transparent about feelings, everyone in my family just ignored them or acted them out. If I had developed the tools to identify my feelings, I absolutely believe that my relationship history would have looked very different.

A major saboteur to effectively grieving the breakup of a relationship is telling yourself that you can just "hook up" with your ex for old times' sake and that you will be okay. That is a delusional lie! If you are playing the "It's over, it's over… come on over!" game, then you have neither emotionally nor physically severed the tie. Hanging out with the ex in any form will set your progress back, and you will experience the same pain all over again. Cut the cord and breathe on your own. You need at least three months of absolutely *no contact* with your old squeeze before you are ready to move on. Yes, you read it correctly: I said NO CONTACT.

Get Rid of Your Old Stash

Keeping the contact information for all your old dates and relationships is like an alcoholic who is trying to stop drinking but keeps a bottle in the trunk of his car…just in case. If a relationship ended, then it ended for a reason. You do not need to maintain a friendship with someone who broke your heart or whose heart you may have broken. Hopefully, you have other friends who can help you through periods of loneliness. If you see your ex in the grocery store, of course you will want to be adult enough to say "hello" and engage in a conversation of thirty seconds maximum. But following an ex on Facebook, Snapchat, or Instagram is not getting over them. You are literally maintaining a connection that will sustain any remaining pain. Cyberstalking an old flame who dumped you cold or who cheated on you will keep those resentments burning. Looking for a new relationship with a heart filled with resentment is neither a good combination nor a good look. The absence of any contact speeds the healing process. You are not available for a new relationship if you are holding on to an old one. Remember, if you're holding on by just a thread, you're still holding on!

A couple, both in their forties, came into my office for counseling because the guy's phone still had the contact information of every woman he had ever dated. His new girlfriend was not a big fan of his trophy list, and she wanted to know what I thought about it. I asked him how many ex-girlfriends were still in his phone, and he answered that there were around two hundred names. I then asked him how many of those ex-relationships included romps between the sheets, and he answered, "All of them." I had a great deal of difficulty suppressing my astonishment at the sheer number of his sexual escapades and the not-so-professional urge to tell his girlfriend to run for the hills to avoid a sexually transmitted disease.

I did tell them that if he did not erase every one of those names, she needed to end the relationship immediately.

The guy looked like I told him to cut off his right hand as he started claiming that these women were "just friends."

I informed him that unless the girlfriend was absolutely on board with his so-called "friends," the friendships could not be anything but a brief "hello" if he ran into them at the Tom Thumb grocery store.

She cried as Mr. Player stormed out of my office. Needless to say, they never returned.

Get Control of Your Finances and Get Out of Debt

Nothing fuels the desperation for finding Prince Charming quite like financial fears and debt. Here is the truth, Cinderella: If you do not take responsibility for yourself financially, you will throw caution to the wind in searching for the elusive prince. If you *must* find a sugar daddy to rescue you and pay your bills, you'll put up with a lot of unacceptable behavior and settle for less than you really want and deserve.

Looking at someone's big, fat wallet can be intoxicating for a while, but eventually its allure will give way to the reality of who that person is. Think about this scenario: At age forty, you date and marry a wealthy man who's age sixty. Even though collecting Jimmy Choos and traveling the world in a private jet can be sexy for a few years, will the attraction remain when you are fifty-five and he's seventy-five? I can pretty much guarantee that when you crawl into the sack with septuagenarian former Prince Charming, his saggy skin and mushy muscles will not be attractive.

May-December Romances...Not Good!

Several of my wealthy male clients only date women who are much younger than they. These guys wear women on their arms like they wear rings on their fingers, and they typically have a substantial number of discarded arm baubles in their historical jewelry box. Their common illusion is that a decorative young woman will turn them into an Adonis, and they believe other men envy their ability to date young hotties. The problem with this scenario is that the men often tire of these needy women once the initial sexual circus act becomes "ho hum" and the so-called love flame starts to flicker. They then dump the women cold, leaving them heartbroken and panicked, with only a fantasy of being rescued and living in the kingdom. In their attempt to find another aging man in need of their bedroom gymnastics, these women will often turn to Botox, face lifts, tucks, laser treatments, and grotesque lip fillers, which too often make them look like freaks in a circus sideshow.

This cycle can and will suck the life out of you along with your diminishing savings and your fragile self-esteem. Ladies, remember this: IT'S NOBODY'S JOB TO RESCUE YOU! You, in conjunction with your Higher Power, can—and must—rescue yourself!

Allison

"I'm staying home today. I've got 'mood poisoning.'"
—Dania Dbaibo Darwish

Allison was raised in a very strict, fundamental religious home that taught self-sacrifice and taking care of others at your own expense. As missionaries, her parents were sent, with their children, to live in various impoverished developing countries. While her parents were tending to the needs of others, Allison, at age thirteen, was charged with the day-to-day responsibility of taking care of her three younger siblings. If one of her siblings was still hungry after eating their allotted serving of food, Alison was expected to share some of hers. If her siblings awakened during the night, it was Allison's job to soothe and quieten their fears so that her parents could get their much-needed sleep. Anytime Allison wanted something for herself or complained about her role, she was punished and shamed for "being selfish and ungrateful." Living in this difficult environment taught Allison that the way to obtain the approval of both God and her parents was to deny her own personal needs and wants.

The first time I saw Allison as a client, she came as a referral from her psychiatrist. Two months earlier she had been hospitalized because of a suicide attempt. The pain of the breakup between she and Alan, her on-again, off-again boyfriend of a year, had been so devastating that suicide became the only option in her mind. At age twenty-two, she was absolutely desperate to reverse her overwhelming sadness and feelings of worthlessness.

After obtaining some family of origin information along with the assurance that Allison was no longer suicidal, I decided to delve into her social life.

"So, Allison," I said. "Tell me about your relationship with Alan."

"We met in a coffee shop," she began, "and when he smiled at me, I literally got goose bumps all over my body. We chatted for about an hour, and as we were leaving, he asked for my number. The next day, Alan called me—and the rest is history! After two dates, I started thinking Alan could be my future husband. Everything was perfect."

"Why did you guys break up?" I asked.

With tears in her eyes, Allison explained. "One day, after we had been dating for about six months, Alan told me that he thought it would be a good idea for us to date other people. I was absolutely flabbergasted at his suggestion. I mean, I had been the perfect girlfriend. I did his laundry, cooked dinner for him anytime he asked, and always paid for at least half of our entertainment. As a schoolteacher, I'm not wealthy, so that was no easy thing to do. I never told Alan no, I was always available whenever he called, and I never took any time to myself, even if I was exhausted. How could I have been a better girlfriend? I just don't understand."

As Allison started to sob, I handed her a tissue (I keep a plentiful supply), and after giving her a few moments to release her deep sadness, I answered. "Because of your role in your family, you were taught that it's your job and duty to do everything for everyone, even at your own expense. You believe that to get the approval of people you love, you cannot say no. You have no idea how important it is to practice self-care, even if it sometimes feels selfish. As a matter of fact, trying to be little Miss Perfect so that a man or some other authority figure accepts you frequently results in depression.

"It's also important for you to know that Alan wanting to date other people was not about you. It affected you greatly, but it was

about Alan and his issues. You could not have been skinny enough, pretty enough, generous enough, or selfless enough to make Alan want to stay in the relationship. You are lovable and valuable simply because you breathe air, and what others think about you is really none of your business. I am going to teach you how to have a loving relationship with yourself, so that you never again become a sacrificial lamb for anyone."

Chapter 2
It's All About You, Girl—Loving Me Some Me

The Many Shades of Shame

You know the feeling. There's a great possibility, however, that you do not fully understand the meaning and power of shame. The majority of people do not. Even though you may have heard your parents or teachers say to you as a child, "Shame on you!" or "You should be ashamed of yourself!" you were probably unaware of the vast power of those words. All you knew was that it felt awful to be shamed. You walked away from the experience with your head down, shoulders slumped, and tears welling in your eyes.

So what exactly is shame, and how could it feel so humiliating?

Shame is an emotion that tells you that your inner self is somehow defective. It tells you that you are unworthy, dishonorable, and disgraceful. Because shame tends to gnaw and fester in your gut, it will not only make you uncomfortable but will also greatly damage your ability to see yourself as you really are. It creates in you the perception that something is fundamentally wrong within your very being. Although you may act as if you have everything together and the world may perceive you as such, your internal voice whispers, "It is a lie. You are not enough."

As you continue to demean yourself, the shame will grow and become excessive. In its pervasiveness, it will create a deep, gut-wrenching feeling that you are worthless, grossly inadequate, less than, and intrinsically bad. You will start to believe that your very existence is a mistake.

Excessive shame not only uncomfortable but within itself it's toxic and can often become debilitating. As you buy into the message that you are inherently bad, the toxic shame starts to cloud or mask your ability to recognize your true inherent value. You become deluded into believing that your value has been lost or, at best, severely damaged. Picture a diamond that has been covered in mud. Although the diamond's value has not been altered in any way, the mud makes it impossible to recognize the intrinsic value of the diamond. Toxic shame is the mud that impairs your ability to know your inherent value.

Toxic shame will sabotage your ability to live life with spontaneity, joy, and authenticity, thus depleting you of vitality and energy. In order to compensate for the belief that your essence is not enough, you will subconsciously determine that you must act as if you are one of those whom you perceive as being adequate so that you are acceptable in the eyes of others. If you are acceptable to others, you can then accept yourself. Because it's uncomfortable being in your own skin, you will develop the ability to become a chameleon depending upon the circumstances. Like a kite blowing in the wind, you will flail this way and that, depending upon the thinking and feeling reality of others. The continuation of this internal desperate process is absolutely exhausting.

In response to feeling ashamed, less than, or inferior, you will either stay in a place of inferiority or develop defense mechanisms that will delude you into believing that you are superior to others. Judgment, criticism, aggressiveness, and self-righteous indignation are some of the ways you may try to cover up your feelings of unworthiness or shame. Saying to yourself, "I am better than others," will temporarily ease the misery of shame. However, the relief will not last, and the cover-up behaviors will continue.

Somewhere around four months of age, my first grandchild, Owen, started smiling—really smiling! When he smiled, every speck of his body radiated joy. His eyes would crinkle, his arms and legs would flail, and his fingers and toes would curl simultaneously. Of course, his joy was contagious because it was literally impossible for me or anyone else to not answer his smiles with smiles of our own.

One day as I relished watching Owen in the deliciousness of his joy, it dawned on me: this is how we were all created. We were created to exude an almost irrepressible, spontaneous joy for simply living as who we are, a pure and untainted joy that affords us the freedom to play.

So what happened to inhibit your capacity for this sort of boundless joy? Your thoughts were contaminated by the shame messages and the defeatism of others.

Humility enables you to see yourself in true relation to others. You understand that you are not better than any other human being. Humility facilitates your ability to embrace your humanity, keeping you mindful of your need for a power greater than yourself. Both the awareness of your connection to a Higher Power and the awareness of your connection to mankind are in themselves spiritual experiences.

As you begin to understand shame and recognize its presence in your life, it is important for you to be able to differentiate between guilt and shame. While shame is about your inner self and your perception of your value, guilt is about your outer self—your words and actions. Guilt is a valuable emotion because it is a warning sign that you may have acted outside of your value system. When you feel guilty about something, stop and ask yourself if you have said or done anything abusive or contrary to your values. If the answer is yes, make an apology, change your behavior, and then leave it alone. If you continue to feel guilty, you're probably feeling shame rather than guilt.

Remember to separate your actions from your value. When identifying offenses to others, it's valuable that you know you are not responsible for their feelings and actions. You are responsible *to* other people—to be honest and to be kind. Being honest means not lying, and being kind means not being abusive. (Saying, "No" is not unkind. Saying, "No, you jerk" is unkind).

Here are some of the many ways you may have experienced shame as a child or young adult, which then skewed your vision of Mr. Marvelous.

Parental Shaming

Without a doubt, your parents or other primary caregivers had the most significant influence on the way you learned to view your value. From the moment of your birth, you looked to your parents for sustenance, acceptance, and approval. Your parents were the barometers that revealed your value to you.

It must be stressed that both parents need to avoid shaming a child. If one of the parents sends a child shame-based messages and the other parent sits silently watching, the silent parent is in essence confirming the shameful message. There are many possible ways that parents can shame a child; these are discussed in the next chapter.

School Shaming

Teachers and school administrators also have a powerful influence on a child's perception of self. School authority figures often label children by using shameful messages such as:

- Good versus bad
- Smart versus stupid
- Successful versus a failure

Many times, children are only acknowledged when they are high achievers. This sets them up for performance esteem and perfectionism. It can establish in a child's mind that they are less valuable if they do not measure up to the criteria established by the schools.

Our school systems, for the most part, place more emphasis on high achievement in an academic classroom than artistic endeavors such as art, music, drama, and craftsmanship. In this sort of environment, a child who is more right-brained is considered less valuable than a child who is more left-brained. If you had any sort of learning difference, then you probably got a double whammy—not only did you perform below perfection, but you also needed extra help to learn a concept or additional time to complete a task.

Another factor to consider is that a child in a highly academic school may regard anything less than an A as being bad. Making one or more Cs, which is still a passing grade, is regarded by many schools and parents as inadequate.

If you were expected to make all As, then I am sure you felt a lot of pressure. This sort of pressure creates a shaming, stress-filled academic experience instead of an esteeming, pleasurable learning experience.

It is also very important that teachers are careful about the emotional abuse of children in regard to humiliating and embarrassing children in front of their peers. I know of a third-grade teacher who used the shortest girl and tallest boy in her class as examples of the meaning of short and tall. She told the two children to stand in front of the class as she talked about the difference in their size. The children felt embarrassed as their classmates giggled. Even as an adult, the student who was used to represent short still remembers that experience as being emotionally painful and shaming.

Another example is that of a fourth-grade teacher who put up a bulletin board in his classroom stating that one of the students (the teacher actually used the student's name) was the world's biggest procrastinator. I saw this student as a client when she was in college. One of her difficulties was procrastination, and it was greatly affecting her ability to complete her degree. The young adult had literally fulfilled the prophecy that the teacher had so insensitively created.

Both situations were horribly shameful. The children were used in ways that were demeaning and humiliating. There is absolutely no place in a classroom for the shaming of children. If parents are aware of this type of behavior, they should absolutely intervene.

Religious Shaming

Religious leaders, Sunday school teachers, and parents intensely influence a child's perception of self. When this is done in negative ways, it produces deep shame. Some examples of negative religious influences are:

- Fanaticism
- Rigidity
- The concept of being born unworthy
- Conditional acceptance and love from God
- Spiritual superiority

Religious shame is horrifically damaging to a child/emerging adult's self-esteem. It can be one of the most destructive and difficult to heal of all the shaming messages. It erodes an individual at the very core of his being. If one perceives that he is unworthy in the eyes of his Higher Power, then he will continually view himself as being inadequate. In his perception, he was doomed at the moment of his birth and can never sufficiently right the wrong.

A spiritually narcissistic person is convinced their religious beliefs are the only way. Their viewpoint excludes anyone else's right to think differently and creates an individual who is spiritually "one up" and thinks of themselves as superior. If you were taught that your church possessed the only true belief system that is honored by God, you will tend to assert that those who believe differently are condemned. This can create a sense of spiritual insecurity as you may have tried to reconcile how an all-loving Higher Being can doom any of his or her children to eternal exile. Both as a child and as an adult you believe, "If it can happen to another, it can certainly happen to me."

If you experienced religious shame as a child, you may have a very difficult time developing a healthy concept of a Higher Power or God. Because I believe that self-esteem and a belief in an all-loving Higher Power go hand in hand, it is important to clear away your childhood concept of God and start over. You will need to create an image of a Higher Power or God who does not judge, punish, or send difficulties to you or anyone else. You will have to learn to trust that your Higher Power wants only the best for you and all other human beings. You must truly believe that your Higher Power looks at you and thinks, *You rock just because you exist!*

Because of the lasting impact of religious shame, I have found that it is often easier to help an atheist create a concept of a loving Higher Power than it is to help a victim of religious abuse re-create and accomplish the same task. Those old-time religious shame messages have claws that dig deeply into a person's soul and wrap tentacles of self-loathing around a person's heart and mind.

Societal Shaming

Societal shaming occurs when a group of individuals collectively views others as "less than." This can be done through judgment based on the following:

- Racism
- Sexism
- Homophobia
- Adoration of physical perfectionism

A child who is judged because of his race, gender, sexual orientation, or physical features will start to believe that he was created inferior, bad, or less than. Because a child cannot change how he was created, the child will develop "existence shame" and become toxic to himself. He believes that his very existence is a mistake.

As a result of the child's self-perception that he is defective, the child will feel the need to overcompensate. This is usually done in one of two ways: either the child acts out, thus creating within himself an illusion of power, or the child becomes submissive and attempts to become the person he thinks the superior class needs and wants him to be. It is a type of gang mentality. The child or adolescent thinks, *Alone I am nothing. But if I associate with you and your power, I will become something.*

The child throws caution to the wind because the need to belong will override his ability to make decisions that are in his best interest. The defenses against societal judgment cause him to deny the reality of who he is. Self-denial puts the child in a continual state of self-hate and will often create great animosity and aggression toward the self and others.

Personal Relationship/Friendship Shaming

As a child begins to socialize, the opinions of peers gain a great deal of importance. Being considered "one of the group" establishes a feeling of internal safety for a child when he is around other children. As social beings, we were created to be in fulfilling relationships. Friendships satisfy our need to belong and add a joyful dimension to life, regardless of age.

If you were ridiculed, teased, or bullied, you were the recipient of personal relationship/friendship shaming. This behavior could have been traumatic for you in that your safety (physical and/or emotional) was threatened. Because of the importance of belonging to a peer group and the fear of the offensive behavior escalating, you may have been hesitant to tell a responsible adult about what you were experiencing. As a result, you probably believed that there was no one to rescue you if you needed rescuing. It was scary. In order to compensate for the fear, you may have become shy and antisocial or aggressive toward others. You felt lonely and sad and you just knew that you did not belong.

Creating Shame within a Child: Meet the Parents

Hopefully you now have a working understanding of the meaning of shame, the meaning of self-esteem, and the sources of shame. You may also find yourself embracing the truth of the inherent worth of yourself and others. If you are, then great! If not, hang in there. More will be revealed. At any rate, most people start to ask the question, "How does this distortion of reality begin?"

The answer is, "Through ineffective parenting and caregiving."

Ineffective parenting, or the inability of caregivers to root and establish a healthy self-esteem system, leaves a deep wound within a child. Unless the wound is healed, it will remain throughout childhood and continue into adulthood, sustaining the illusion within the individual that he is less valuable than others. This illusion will create a feeling of insecurity and will interfere with his ability to care for self and others.

If your parents lacked a healthy sense of self-esteem, they simply could not have given you what they didn't have as children. It is like attempting to pour milk from an empty pitcher. Your parents/caregivers were unable to nurture within you what they did not realize within themselves. Because of that, your needs were never fully met, and your self-esteem was never adequately rooted. Thus, the wounds that were formed within your parents were passed down and established within the next generation—you. This generational shame is like a runaway train wreaking internal havoc within family members from generation to generation until someone stops the cycle.

Over time, these wounds become larger and result in the creation of a shame core within a child. In other words, a child subconsciously believes to the very core of his being that he is inadequate. This shame core will continue to worsen and will be sustained by the internalization of toxic shame messages. As this happens, the child begins to perceive himself as having very little value. In reality, the child's self-esteem is not lost; it is merely masked.

It is important to remember that one's intrinsic value from birth is absolutely present and permanent. It is the *recognition* of one's value that becomes distorted and lost.

Without a doubt, the great majority of parents, including your parents, do the best job they can possibly do. Their intentions are pure. They believe with all their hearts that they are parenting effectively and with a tremendous amount of love. Unfortunately, love does not always equate to effective parenting. Most people parent as they were parented, without realizing that what they are doing is creating emotional wounds deep within the spirit of the child.

As you read about shameful parenting techniques, please focus on yourself as a child as opposed to the ways you may have parented your own children. Remember, the realization of your own woundedness and resulting shame are the beginning of healing. After you connect with yourself as a child, you will then be able to parent your own children differently. If your children are adults, you will be able to make amends to them and help them to break the cycle of generational shame. These deep childhood wounds and the resulting shame core can be formed in the following ways.

Mixed Messages

Mixed messages are created when a parent's or caregiver's words and actions are incongruent. This experience is very confusing to a child. Most children do not have the ability or courage to address this incongruence with their caregiver for fear of being considered disrespectful. Many of us grew up being told that it was not OK to question adults. As a result, we learned to dismiss and repress what we were experiencing. We learned to deny ourselves. Whenever a child's reality is denied, his self-esteem takes a hit. The fallout for the continuation of this sort of experience is an inadequate sense of self-value.

Mixed messages that you may have experienced:

- "You are such a good boy/girl."

If you grew up hearing this statement, you got the message that you had the possibility of being bad. Remember, there is no such thing as a bad child. A more effective statement would be, "You are such a precious child, and that can never change." I often hear people refer to a baby who cries as being a bad baby. My body cringes when I hear that statement. It is totally illogical because babies are supposed to cry. It is their only means of communication. Although I realize that the adult does not intend to be offensive, the energy that accompanies the concept of a baby being good or bad depending upon whether the baby sleeps easily or cries is negative. Eliminating the statements that contribute to a negative self-image within a child is an effective way to foster a solid sense of self.

- As a parent was about to discipline you as a child, he states, "This hurts me more than it does you."

This statement was demeaning to you because it discounted your own pain while it elevated the adult's pain. A more effective statement would be, "I love you very much, and I know that you feel sad about being in trouble with me."

Withdrawal of Physical or Emotional Affection

When a parent withdraws physical or emotional affection because of the child's behavior, the child internalizes the message that his unacceptable behavior has reduced his value in the eyes of the parent. Children cannot be responsible for owning their internal value, because the total transference from other esteem to self-esteem does not happen until young adulthood. The child must look to the parent or caregiver as his primary source for value validation.

The child believes that if his parents see him as lovable, then he must be lovable. Likewise, the child believes that if his parents do *not* see him as lovable, then he must not be lovable. Withdrawal of affection is read as withdrawal of love. The parent has not separated the child's behavior from his value. This has an extremely damaging effect on the child's solidification and realization of self-esteem.

Examples of physical or emotional withdrawal that you may have experienced:

- Your parent said, "You are very bad for hitting your sister."

In this situation, your parent was withdrawing emotional nurturing by telling you that you were bad. A nurturing response would be, "Your behavior is not OK, and you must stop hitting your sister. You are valuable and precious even though you have misbehaved. Your value can never change."

- Your parent was unwilling to hug you after reprimanding you for unacceptable behavior.

This sent you a disapproving message of your essence, which you internalized as being less valuable. Although a hug should not be forced upon a child, it is important for a parent to be willing to hug the child even when the parent is unhappy with the child's behavior. A parent can ask the child if he wants a hug or say to the child, "Even though I am angry and I do not like what you have done, I would love to hug you and remind you of your preciousness."

Physical Neglect

Physical neglect can take several forms. Most commonly, it is not meeting the child's need for physical attention or affection. Meeting the child's physical needs determines how the child's body develops and thrives.

Children are incapable of caring for themselves physically, so it is vitally important that parents model healthy physical self-care. Habits that are established throughout childhood will be carried into adulthood and will greatly affect a person's physical health throughout his lifetime.

Equally as important as physical attention is physical affection. If you did not receive a lot of physical affection, you learned to doubt your lovability. Lovability equates to value.

People will say that they know their parents loved them even though they were rarely hugged as children. I always ask them how they knew that they were lovable if their parents did not show them. Remember, children need words and behaviors to be congruent. Even though some adolescents do not like to be hugged, they like for their parents to want to hug them. It is never appropriate, however, to force a child to hug or to be hugged by anyone.

Physical neglect also includes not setting appropriate limits for the child. Because children do not naturally set appropriate limits for themselves, a major part of functional parenting is saying no to children when they want to do things that are not in their best interest. A parent's difficulty in setting limits with a child is usually the result of a parent wanting to avoid conflict. A parent can have trouble dealing with their own feelings appropriately and not want to risk disapproval from the child or adolescent.

To be effective in setting limits, a parent must be able to handle the child's feelings of anger or sadness in having to deal with boundaries. The parent should always operate in the child's best interest, even when the child is resistant. Chances are the child is not going to say, "Gee, Dad. Thanks for persisting in asking me to go to bed." While resistance from children and adolescents is normal and may not be particularly fun, the parent must learn to persevere with setting limits. Children feel valued when they have limits.

Examples of physical neglect that you may have experienced:

- Your parents did not teach you about personal grooming.

Personal grooming helps a child learn to honor his body by keeping it clean and healthy. As you entered into adolescence, you began to look to your peers rather than your parents for self-validation. Desiring to "fit in" is normal for an adolescent, and eliminating body odor, grungy teeth, dirty fingernails, and facial hair (for boys) helps to remove reasons for ridicule and exclusion from peers. Personal grooming is a life skill that the child will take into adulthood, and it will affect his ability to thrive, both socially and professionally.

- Your parents did not feed you healthy food and/or allowed you to overindulge in foods high in fat and sugar.

If left to your own childhood desires, you probably would have lived on greasy french fries and other high-fat foods. Most children will choose pizza over broccoli and ice cream over a glass of milk. Fats and sugar taste good. Teaching a child moderation in regard to eating high-fat and sugary foods will allow the child to enjoy occasional indulgences without becoming controlled by extreme eating behaviors and the potential health issues that may occur as a result. I believe that one of the most covertly abusive behaviors in our culture is a parent allowing a child to eat himself into obesity.

- Your parents did not ensure that you had enough physical activity.

I am not one of those people who believes that television and video games are intrinsically bad. It is important, however, that a child engages in daily moderate physical activity in order to facilitate energy and a sense of well-being.

- Your parents did not set limits on the amount of your physical activities or they pushed you too hard in physical activities.

There is a trend in our culture of involving children in too many extracurricular sporting activities at the expense of any downtime. Along with activities, it is good for children to learn to relax and do nothing.

- Your parents did not take you to the dentist or doctor.
- Your parents allowed you to stay up as late as you wanted.

Sleep is essential for growing bodies—and positive attitudes.

Abandonment (Physical and Emotional)

Abandonment is when a parent or caregiver leaves a child physically or is emotionally unavailable.

Physical Abandonment

Children are self-centered by nature and often believe that they are the cause of situations that happen to their parents. For example, if your parents got divorced or separated, you may have assumed that in some way you caused the rift. It's essential that children be told that a parent is not leaving because of the children or the children's behavior.

In the case of a parent's death, the same message applies. This message should be repeated many times. With divorce or separation, it is also extremely important that the parent who is not living with the children take every opportunity to spend time with them. Children need to know that they are loved very much by both parents, that their needs will be met, and that they are safe.

Children may also feel abandoned if one or both parents work away from the home or travel frequently. If this is the case, it is crucial that the children receive nurturing care from whoever takes over for the parents during these times. It is also important for parents to be attentive to the children when the parents are at home, reassuring the children that they are loved very much.

Emotional Abandonment

Emotional abandonment is the unwillingness or inability of a parent to address his own feelings or the feelings of his child. It could be that a parent is denying his own feelings or is so wrapped up in his own emotions that he fails to notice or be sensitive to what is going on with the child.

Examples of emotional abandonment that you may have experienced:

- You saw that your parent was crying, you asked what was wrong, and your parent said, "Nothing is wrong."

When a parent does not acknowledge the reality of what he or she is feeling, the child learns to doubt his own reality. The child sees and interprets the obvious, and yet his parent denies the obvious. Who is the child to believe, himself or his parent? Parents, in the mind of a child, represent truth and authority. Therefore, the child determines that his truth must be incorrect. This sets up the child for a pattern of self-doubt and negates his ability to trust his gut or birth-created intuition.

An effective response would be, "I am feeling sad. This is my sadness, and I will take care of it. It is OK for people to feel sad."

- Your parent noticed that you were feeling sad, fearful, or happy, and they did not comment on or talk about your emotions.

When parents do not notice the feelings of a child, the child feels unloved and will, therefore, conclude that he must be unlovable. Remember that in order for a child to root healthy self-esteem, he must understand, by seeing and hearing, that his parents regard him as being extremely valuable and lovable. Noticing and verbally acknowledging a child's feelings are effective ways to nurture and root a child's value to the child.

An effective comment would be, "It looks to me like you are feeling afraid. Can I give you a hug, and would you like to talk about it?"

- Your parents did not tell you that they loved you.

It is extremely important that both parents tell children that they love them. Oftentimes, people will say, "My child knows that I love him even if I don't say it," or "I know that my father or mother loved me although I never heard them say it."

Loving actions are absolutely not enough. When parents do not *tell* their child that they love him, the child will harbor a deep-rooted doubt that he is lovable. A child will hear the words "I love you" spoken between other people, and he will subconsciously or consciously question why his parents do not say that to him. The child will easily conclude that there must be something wrong with him to cause his parent not to speak the words, "I love you." Children need to hear the words "I love you" from their parents and primary caregivers, and they need to hear it often and whole-heartedly!

- Your parent was walled off from his or her own emotions and did not feel, demonstrate, or talk about them.

Emotions are "energy in motion." When a parent does not appropriately acknowledge and feel his emotions, the unacknowledged emotional energy will ooze into the environment rather than disappearing. Because a child is an emotional sponge, he will absorb the emotional energy of the parent, store it internally, claim the emotion as his own, and then feel the emotions of the parent and for the parent.

The child may feel these emotions either during childhood or later in life, but trust me, they will be felt at some time during the child's life.

This often occurs when a parent suffers from depression. Depression is deep sadness, fear, or anger, and even though these feelings have been stuffed and not acknowledged, they are omnipresent in the home environment. The child absorbs the unfelt feelings, internalizes the depressive energy, and develops his own case of depression or anxiety. It is the perfect storm that is re-created within the child. When a client comes into my office and presents with depression or anxiety, I ask which parent or grandparent had depression or anxiety when the client was growing up. We can always trace it back to someone in the family.

The same scenario is true when parents spew their feelings inappropriately into the environment. A child will absorb the spewed feelings, internalize them as his own, and then act them out at some point. Rage is a good example of this. Rage is the behavioral result of accumulated anger that has not been appropriately acknowledged and felt. The anger seethes internally and simply reaches a boiling point. The pressure cooker explodes. As a result, a child will absorb the toxic anger energy and then act it out. People will frequently credit their rage issues to having a "bad temper." It is as if they inherited the temper genetically like the color of their eyes. People are not born with flaring tempers. They absorb flaring toxic energy and then claim it as their own.

On the other hand, a parent who is connected with his own emotional reality and allows himself to experience his emotions without shame will be able to feel his feelings appropriately. This will prevent a child from absorbing the parent's feelings and will also provide a model for appropriate "feeling behavior." For example, a parent who is feeling anger should say to a child, "I am feeling angry. This is my anger, not yours, and I will handle it. It does not mean that I do not love you. I am simply angry."

- Your parents told you that your feelings were wrong and should not be felt, perhaps telling you that you should not cry, feel angry, or feel afraid.

Feelings, or emotions, are a very important part of every person's identity, and it's essential that children be allowed to identify and feel their feelings. Feelings that are ignored, shamed, or resisted do not disappear; they actually remain inside one's being and will build upon themselves. As the feelings build, they are then often expressed inappropriately.

When feelings are shamed, a child is shamed. As a defense against the shame, a child will learn to disconnect from his feelings, thus disconnecting from himself. Typically, boys are shamed for expressing fear or sadness, while girls are shamed for expressing anger. When feelings are appropriately acknowledged and expressed, however, they will lose power and will not adversely affect a person mentally or physically. Because a child will instinctively express what he is feeling, it is imperative that parents/caregivers teach ways to appropriately express feelings.

An effective parenting statement would be, "It looks like you are feeling sad, and that is absolutely all right. Would you like to talk about it?"

Emotional Incest

Emotional incest is using a child to support or improve a parent's emotional needs. The child is given the message that their job is to make a parent feel proud, happy, safe, etc. Your parents' job was to take care of your emotional needs by nurturing you with love, validation, and support so that you could focus on age-appropriate activities and relationships.

Emotional incest causes a child to be enmeshed with his parent. This means that there is no separateness. The parent believes that he is a reflection of the child's feelings and behaviors, and the child is a reflection of the parent's feelings and behaviors. It is not uncommon for an adult to assume that if his parent committed a crime or committed suicide, then he is doomed to a similar behavior. Emotional incest is very detrimental to a child because if a child is parenting his parent, then he is being robbed of his emotional childhood. Not only is the child prevented from being a child emotionally but the parent is not available to focus on parenting the child.

Examples of emotional incest that you may have experienced:

- You misbehaved and your parent made a statement such as, "I feel so disappointed in you. I cannot believe that you would do this to me."

An appropriate parenting statement would be, "It is not OK to hit your sister, and I feel angry. It is my anger and I will deal with it. I do want that behavior to stop."

- Your father said to you, "I am going out of town and you need to take care of your mother and keep her happy."

An appropriate parenting statement would be, "I am going out of town. Your mom will be here to take care of you. I hope you have a good couple of days."

- Your parents got their feelings hurt because you wanted to spend time with your friends rather than with them. In this case, you were expected to keep your parents from feeling sad or lonely.
- Your parents expected you to behave in a way that was beyond your capability because of age or cognitive development.
- Your parents needed you to behave in a certain way so that they could feel happy rather than angry or embarrassed. Examples of this are: taking you, as a three-year-old, out to a prolonged dinner event and expecting you to sit still and be quiet; expecting

you at two years old not to touch items on a coffee table; expecting you and your siblings not to have disagreements; expecting you to be responsible for your siblings.

- Your parents said, "I am so disappointed in you."

This is an extremely shaming message; it rips the child to the core of his essence. It tells the child that he has failed to fulfill his duty to make his parent feel happy or proud.

It is not the child's job to make his parent feel anything.

Emotional incest is particularly shame producing because the task set before the child is impossible. Adults are responsible for their own emotional reality. When a child is unable to satisfy a parent's emotional needs, he will feel extremely sad or guilty because he has failed at creating happiness, pride, or love in his parents, the people whom he loves the most. That's a monumental job and can produce a lot of fear within the child because he is emotionally and physically dependent on his parents for survival. It's like water-skiing behind a boat that no one is driving! If he cannot please his parents, the child fears possible withdrawal of the attention and love he so desperately needs, thus creating a fear of abandonment that will be carried into adulthood.

Emotional incest also causes a child to feel inadequate and like a failure. It creates the need to be an emotional care-taker, a people pleaser, and a dutiful son/daughter. The child will believe that it is his job to "fix" anyone who is feeling

44

sadness, fear, anger, guilt, or shame. He will absorb the uncomfortable feelings of family and friends, perceive these feelings as being his own, and then make behavioral choices based on the absorbed feelings.

The child learns to live life from a place of *duty* as opposed to living life from a place of *choice*. These dutiful roles will continue into adulthood and will sabotage the ability to create healthy relationships. People who are overly dutiful will also be unable to feel a general sense of happiness independent from the well-being of others. Their ability to live a satisfying life will be impeded.

It is never, ever a child's job to take care of a parent emotionally!

Physical Caretaking of a Parent, Grandparent, or Other Adult

Sometimes a child may be used to physically nurture or physically take care of a parent, grandparent, or other adult. This most frequently occurs when the adult suffers from debilitating depression, physical impairment, drug addiction, or chronic mental or physical disease.

Examples of physical caretaking that you may have experienced:

- Your parent or other adult expected you to make him physically comfortable.

- You spent time grooming your parent or other adult by brushing their hair, changing their clothing, bathing them, or changing their adult diaper.
- You spent time sustaining a parent or other adult's health by dispensing their medication or vitamins, exercising them, or taking them to the restroom.
- You gave your parents or other adults foot rubs.
- You fed your parent or other adult.

Like emotional incest, physical caretaking of an adult sets up the child for failure, as the task is beyond the child's capability.

This does *not* include a child helping with small tasks within the family unit or having assigned chores. Family chores that everyone does are more about participating within a system as opposed to feeling personally responsible for an adult's physical well-being.

An adult may find it necessary to take care of an aging parent or another adult physically. This, too, is different from a child taking care of a parent.

Perfectionism

Perfectionism is a parent's desire for a child to look perfect, act perfectly, and perform perfectly. Even though the parents do not acknowledge their own imperfections or inappropriate behaviors, they expect perfection from their child.

Examples of perfectionism that you may have experienced:

- You brought home a report card with a B+ and your parents complained that you did not make an A.
- You were not allowed to leave the house without your room being perfectly picked up and your bed perfectly made.
- Your parents often fought and yelled at each other, while expecting you and your siblings to always get along and not fight with each other.
- Your parents constantly criticized your physical appearance or insisted that you always look a particular way.

Expecting a child/emerging adult to attain an idealized state articulated by the parent impedes him from accepting himself as being real or human. As a result, the child is in a continual state of feeling less than. He becomes like a gerbil in a wheel, always in motion while attempting to do everything better. Because perfection cannot be obtained and sustained, he will learn to do what he perceives he should be doing rather than what he wants to be doing. He becomes frustrated and feels grossly inadequate. He will be hesitant to attempt new endeavors because if he cannot do something perfectly, then he must be a failure. He may also develop a tendency to procrastinate. In order to cope with the shame that results from the inability to achieve perfection, the child learns to focus on and criticize the imperfections of self and others. This character trait will remain throughout adulthood and will sabotage relationships.

Part of being human is doing things imperfectly and learning to do things differently the next time. If a child is taught to exchange the word "mistake" for the words "learning experience," a shameful or negative connotation can be replaced with something positive and esteeming. Pia Mellody calls the concept of embracing our flawed humanity as being created "perfectly imperfect." This is an important part of self-esteem. Children will develop an attitude of self-acceptance by seeing and hearing a parent's self-acknowledgment of his own imperfections as well as the parent giving the child permission to be perfectly imperfect.

Now that we've explored self-esteem, shame, and the sources of shame, you may find yourself realizing that you have some work to do in order to the heal a few childhood wounds. This is vitally important in you quest to finding Mr. Marvelous, so that you do not settle for someone less than what you deserve and desire. In my book, *The Shame Game: Leaving Shame to Live in Abundance*, I include activities at the end of each chapter that can help you identify and start to eliminate the shame in your dating game. I also strongly urge you to make an appointment with a therapist trained in guiding people down the path of healing.

Put Down Those Pom Poms

If you were raised in a family system that taught it was your job to make your parents, grandparents, or teachers happy, you probably struggle with being a people pleaser. People pleasing is when you need *other people* to be happy so that *you* can be happy. Wanting the people that you love to be happy is human, but when it becomes a need, you will eventually lose your ability to say no along with your ability to take care of yourself.

Saying no was a very difficult thing for me to learn. I often said yes when I wanted to say no because my sense of value was tied to the approval of others. Along with learning to walk around with a plastered smile on my face, I learned to perform at a very high level in school. I vividly remember being in the third grade when the music teacher asked me to sing a solo of the "Battle Hymn of the Republic" before the entire student body. I didn't really want to do it, but because I was such a people pleaser, I agreed. The performance went okay and my parents were thrilled, but singing the words, "in the glory of his *bosom*," was mortifying for me as a ten-year-old girl. For months, the boys teased be relentlessly because I sang the word "bosom."

At age thirteen, I learned that along with earning really good grades, getting votes could be a new way of gaining recognition. I successfully achieved my new goal of being elected cheerleader each year of junior high school and high school. Winning those elections provided me with exactly what I wanted and needed—a very tangible way for me to externalize my sense of value and to feel good about myself.

After getting my divorce at age forty-four, I finally put down my pom poms and gave up my need for the approval of others. It was not that I did not want people to like and admire me; I simply no longer needed their votes. This level of emotional freedom has made a gigantic difference in my life. I no longer believe that it is my job to please others, to try and fix people outside of a professional context, and I can be okay even when the people I love are not okay. As difficult as that can be at times, I now understand that my friends, husband, children, and grandchildren have a God—and it is not me.

I Love Me Some Me!

Years ago, when I was in the process of getting a divorce, Dallas Cowboy football player Terrell Owens would end his media interviews with the proclamation, "I love me some me!" When I first heard him making this bold statement, I criticized him as being arrogant and egotistical. Not only had I been taught that it was selfish and self-centered to love myself, but it was unimaginable that anyone would publicly proclaim "self-love." After I started seriously working on myself, however, I realized that to eliminate my need to be rescued, I had to learn how to "love me some me."

The pathway to learning how to love yourself begins by learning how to enjoy your own company. Have a date night with yourself once a week. Rent a good movie, eat popcorn and frozen yogurt, take a bubble bath, or put a beauty mask on your face. At first, these feelings of loneliness can be uncomfortable, so allow yourself to sit in the feelings without judgment and let the feelings dissipate.

Before getting my divorce, I had very little tolerance for being alone and still. Because I was such an activity junkie, I could not imagine why anyone would choose to do anything by themselves. I literally used to feel sorry for people who were eating alone in a restaurant. I just assumed that this was a last resort and that they were either losers or loners. I know that sounds snobby and naïve, and it just shows that I had no clue how much fun I could have alone with myself.

During and after my divorce, however, all of that changed. I learned to eat alone at restaurants (even some really nice restaurants) and actually enjoy the experience. I not only learned to tolerate being alone, I learned to *love* doing some things alone. Two decades later, I still take time to plan activities with myself. I've been to Hawaii, California, Florida, Austin, and our lake house alone. I always stay at lovely hotels, and I exercise, shop, write, read, and get lots of sleep. Sounds fun, right?

You may have heard people say that the best way to get over the pain of losing a relationship is to get into another relationship. Don't buy it! Jumping into another relationship is like an alcoholic jumping from vodka to gin when what you and the alcoholic really need is to abstain from both. Emotionally detoxing from the last relationship is essential for you to move on down the cafeteria line of men. If you don't take the time "to be," you will continue to sustain your ineffective dating patterns, and, therefore, you will continue to get the same results. If nothing changes, nothing changes. Learning to be comfortable in your own skin will keep you from settling for less than what you want in a relationship.

Say Hello to Self-Esteem

Like shame, people often talk about self-esteem without having a clue as to its real meaning. People will say that someone has either a lot of self-esteem or very little self-esteem. I cannot begin to tell you how often a parent will bring a troublesome adolescent into my office and say something like, "I think the problem is that my child has no self-esteem. If you will just get him to make better grades or realize how great he is at football (or some other activity), then he will have self-esteem."

In reality, self-esteem has nothing to do with accomplishments, beauty, or talent. Self-esteem is different from self-confidence in that self-confidence comes from realizing and believing that you have a particular talent, ability, or unique physical, emotional, or intellectual quality. Self-esteem, on the other hand, is simply knowing with absolute certainty that you are inherently valuable. As you see and love yourself as you truly are, you will experience self-respect, self-interest, and a sense of self-love. In essence, self-esteem is the opposite of shame.

When you were born, your value was established. This is true for everyone. That means that there are no bad people. There are people who behave in ways that are hurtful to others, but their behavior is separate from their birth-established value. If you were to stand at the window of a hospital nursery, it would be impossible to pick out the "bad" or "worthless" babies. That is because there is no such thing. Every child is created precious and worthy. It is important to recognize this truth so that you can truly believe in your own birth-created value.

If you believe that there is any chance whatsoever that any human being can be inherently less valuable than any other human being, you will subconsciously hold on to the possibility that *you* just might be the one created with less value. This possibility will reside deep within your spirit and will impede your ability to believe in the divine value of human beings. Consequently, and most importantly, it will sabotage your ability to embrace the essence of your own value, thus diminishing your self-esteem.

What is interesting about your perception of being "less than" is that it is merely an illusion. You have been conditioned into believing a lie. The reality is that your pre-established value can never be less and has no need to be more. Your value is whole, complete, and static.

Your parents or primary caregivers played an essential role in rooting your concept of self-value or self-esteem. A parent's role is to nurture a child with care, love, and limit-setting so that the child's value is sustained and recognizable to the child. The result is that the child feels safe. Such caregiving and nurturing validates the child's esteem on a very basic level. This functional parenting process confirms the preciousness that already exists within the child.

Additionally, your parents' own self-esteem further developed and sustained your value tank. A parent who comes to know his own preciousness in the eyes of God will then be able to transfer this knowing to the child. As the child gets older, his self-esteem will thrive and come into the child's awareness. The child begins to understand that he, too, is precious.

Nurturing Love

An essential component in the rooting of self-esteem is nurturing love. Nurturing love sustains the birth-given value of a child and greatly enhances a child's ability to flourish. If your parents received nurturing love from their parents, they would have realized their own intrinsic value, thus enabling them to parent you with nurturing love. Parents with self-esteem are able to express nurturing love with very little difficulty.

"So what is nurturing love?" you may ask. Basically, nurturing love is parenting a child for the sole purpose of filling the child with an unshakable awareness of his own inherent worth. It is that simple. In order for a parent to accomplish this important goal, the parenting process needs to include the following:

- The ability to set limits for the child without the withdrawal of physical or emotional affection
- Meeting the child's physical needs
- Physical and emotional presence of the caregiver

54

- Not using the child to meet the parent's emotional or physical needs
- A parent's acknowledgment of their own imperfections and an ability to allow the child to embrace their own humanness
- Absence of verbal, physical, intellectual, spiritual, or sexual abuse
- Congruency between words and behavior
- The experience and expression of joy within the family

When a child/emerging adult experiences a lack of nurturing love, self-value is masked, shame begins to emerge, and a shame core develops. This process happens through exposure to external influences where shame-based messages are taught.

Caring for Your Body, Mind, and Spirit

Take care of your body, mind, and spirit, not because your body is a seduction tool but because it's *good* for you to do so. Herbal baths, reflexology, and massages are good for your body and are beneficial relaxation techniques. Join a gym, see a nutritionist, or take a meditation class.

Meditation is a very effective way to nurture yourself emotionally. The purpose of meditation is to quiet your busy mind and go from a state of suffering or unrest to a state of joy and bliss. In meditation, you learn to leave the activity of the outside world and enter an internal world of calm. As your mind ceases to obsess, it is unable to take off on a journey of anxiety, worry, and depression. It is no longer living in the past or anticipating the future. It is in the now, which in reality is the only moment that exists. When you live in the now, you are better able to reconnect with your intuition and spiritual self.

If you are unaccustomed to a meditation practice, you may be intimidated by the very thought of meditating. You may find yourself saying, "There is no way I can meditate. I have trouble sitting still, much less learning to concentrate long enough to actually meditate." In actuality, meditation is an easy skill to develop once you understand that it is acquired *one minute at a time*. Meditation is a practice that builds upon itself, so it's important to begin slowly. Rather than criticizing yourself for doing it imperfectly, commend yourself for simply doing it. In a very short time, you'll notice the slowing of your thoughts, and you'll gain an increased awareness of the world around you. The moment you begin a meditation practice, you'll enter into an important aspect of self-care.

There are various categories of meditation including concentrative meditation, which focuses attention on breathing, chanting, or imaging; and mindfulness meditation, which focuses on an awareness of what is occurring in your world. I strongly urge you to investigate these possibilities and see if you discover one that looks appealing.

Meditation will help you to become a "human *being*" as opposed a "human *doing*," and it will help relieve periodic anxiety. Not only will your body and mind benefit, but simply being around people will help with the loneliness. Do not go to these places looking for another Mr. Marvelous unless it has been six months since the breakup. You are not ready!

Another healthy aspect of self-care is creating a spiritual practice. I am not talking specifically about religiosity and attending church, although this can be part of a spiritual practice. I'm referring more to taking time each day to read a daily devotional that can give your mind a positive place to dwell instead of falling down into the "woe is me" self-pity hole. There are oodles of wonderful daily meditation books that can be a gigantic help during the grieving process of a breakup. One of my very favorites is Melody Beattie's *The Language of Letting Go*. I started reading that book in 1990, and I continue to read it every morning. I do this because the principles in the book are just as applicable to me and my life today as they were many years ago. I still need to be reminded of the slogans and concepts that can keep me from unhealthy practices with my husband, friends, children, and grandchildren.

Remember that becoming a total Debbie Downer is not attractive and will keep you from drawing positive people into your world. Your friends and family can be a means of empathetic support for a while, but eventually they will tire of the "waaa, waaa, waaas." They will want to get the heck out of Dodge when they see you coming, along with ignoring your calls when they see your name on their caller ID.

Some people experience clinical depression and severe anxiety after a breakup. If your sleep patterns are disrupted for more than three weeks or you experience high anxiety or panic attacks, you should speak with a therapist. The neurotransmitters in your brain could be out of whack because of the breakup trauma, and therapy could really help. An established practice of good self-care will not only give you an added level of confidence to carry you through the dating process but will also become a lifelong habit.

Self-care and truly knowing yourself is the way to become comfortable in your own skin. If you happen to realize some things about yourself that you would like to change or ways that you would like to improve upon, then go for it. Just do it for yourself and not to seduce some yahoo out there that you think is going to save you from having to grow up and take responsibility for yourself.

Remember, Prince Charming is either dead or in rehab! But Mr. Marvelous is out there, waiting for you.

Carol

"I want a man who is kind and understanding.
Is that too much to ask of a millionaire?"
—Zsa Zsa Gabor

I vividly remember meeting Carol for the *first time. As she entered my office, I was immediately struck by her vibrant personality and her infectious smile. Carol told me that she and her sister were experiencing some conflict, and she wanted my guidance as to how they could peacefully reach an agreement. I saw her three or four times, gave her some conflict resolution tools, and fortunately the two of them were able to repair their relationship.*

I met with Carol several times again when John, her husband, died after experiencing a massive heart attack. We worked on understanding the grief process and the best ways to help her three precious daughters get through the horrific pain of losing the father that they adored.

It had been two years since John's death, and I was really looking forward to seeing Carol and learning how she and her three daughters were doing.

"Hi, Carol," I said. "It's wonderful to see you again. You look beautiful and I guess you're an empty-nester now that all of the girls are in college. How's everyone doing?"

"Actually," replied Carol, "we're all doing okay. The past two years have been difficult and we miss John terribly, but it feels as if we are turning a corner with our grief. Thank you for the contribution you made in John's name to the American Heart Association. That was very generous of you."

"You are so welcome," I replied. "What can I do for you today?"

"Well, first of all, I've gone back to school to get a master's degree in interior design, and my oldest daughter and I are planning on starting a design business together."

"That sounds terrific," I replied. "You will be a great interior designer!"

"Thank you!" said Carol. "I'm really excited about our new endeavor. On another note, I've been thinking about the possibility of going on a date or two. I have a couple of

friends who know men they would like me to meet. The girls are all out of the house, and the loneliness can sometimes feel overwhelming."

"I think that could be really fun for you. So what are you waiting for?"

"I am not exactly sure what is holding me back," said Carol. "I guess my main concern is worrying about is how the girls are going to react to me dating. What if they feel like I am betraying their father?"

"If one or more of your daughters do have some feelings of sadness, anger, or fear about you moving on with your life, their feelings will subside with time," I answered. "This will be another very important part of their grief process as they watch you continuing to live your life, even without their father. As difficult as the process could be for them, it's necessary that you enjoy living your own life. By doing so, you are giving each of your daughters permission to continue to live and enjoy their own lives too."

"I also feel a little bit guilty even thinking about being on a date with another man, much less kissing or having sex with someone," Carol said. "It feels like I am betraying John even though he's passed away. That probably sounds pretty crazy. I definitely know that I do not want to be alone the rest of my life, but

how do I know when I am ready to take this leap?"

"First of all, you're not crazy," I said. "You're going through the acceptance stage of grief as you start to visualize your life with a different man. There are some things that we can discuss that will not only be beneficial in the dating process but will also help you decide whether or not you are ready. You are a beautiful, smart, and very kind woman, and you deserve to share your life with a man, if that is what you desire. I believe with every fiber of my being that John would want that for you. Let's get started."

Chapter 3
Become Who You Want to Be And Get What You Want to Get

Is My Issue Codependency?

There are many definitions for the term *codependency*. I personally prefer the author Melody Beattie's definition the best: a codependent person is one who has let another person's behavior affect him or her, and who is obsessed with controlling that person's behavior.

In my first marriage, I was obsessed with the behavior of my husband, and I tried desperately to control what he did or did not do. Needless to say, he was not a big fan of my arrogant ideas of right and wrong and the ways that I tried to change him. Why would he be? No one enjoys...OK umm...being with someone who is critical and controlling, and since controlling others is an illusion, life is no picnic for the person whose life mission is to straighten out another adult's life. When I learned about codependency, I realized that I had to grow up emotionally and fix my codependency.

If you think that you might have some codependency issues, I encourage you to honestly answer the twenty questions below. Write your "yes" or "no" answer after each question.

Twenty Codependency Questions

1. My good feelings about who I am stem from being liked by you.
2. My good feelings about who I am stem from receiving approval from others.
3. Your struggles affect my serenity.
4. My mental attention is focused on solving your problems or relieving your pain.
5. My mental attention is focused on pleasing you.
6. My mental attention is focused on protecting you.
7. My mental attention is focused on manipulating you to do it my way.
8. My self-esteem is bolstered by solving your problems.
9. My self-esteem is bolstered by relieving your pain.
10. My own hobbies and interest are put aside. My time is spent sharing your interest and hobbies.
11. Your clothing and personal appearance are dictated by my desires, as I feel you are a reflection of me.

12. Your behavior is dictated by my desires as I feel you are a reflection of me.
13. I am not aware of how I feel; I am aware of how you feel.
14. I am not aware of what I want; I ask what you want. If I am not aware, I assume.
15. The dreams I have for my future are linked to you.
16. My fear of rejection determines what I say or do.
17. My fear of your anger determines what I say or do.
18. I use giving as a way of feeling safe in our relationship.
19. My social circle diminishes as I involve myself with you.
20. I value your opinion and ways of doing things more than my own.

Answering "yes" to more than five questions means that, like I discovered about myself, you have some work to do around this issue. The value of understanding and then correcting these ideas and behavior will enable you to date more effectively and do relationships differently. Oh, and by the way, people will like you more and enjoy your company much more!

For more information in determining if codependency is an issue for you, I urge you to read Melody Beattie's book *Codependent No More*.

One of the tools that I implemented in changing my codependent ways was learning to let go. Remember these tips:

To "let go" does not mean to stop caring; it means I can't do it for someone else.

65

To "let go" is not to eliminate people from my life; it is understanding that I cannot control others.

To "let go" is to allow others to learn from the consequences of their own behavior and to stop enabling.

To "let go" is to admit that I am powerless over others, and therefore the outcome of another's behavior is not in my hands.

To "let go" is to make the most of myself and my life without blaming or trying to change others.

To "let go" is to care about others as opposed to caretaking others.

To "let go" is not to fix but to be supportive.

To "let go" is not to judge but to allow others to be human beings.

To "let go" is to stay out of the middle trying to arrange and control outcomes.

To "let go" is not to be protective of other adults but allow others to face their own reality.

To "let go" is to accept rather than deny.

To "let go" is not to nag, scold, or argue but instead to discover and acknowledge my own shortcomings and focus on fixing those.

To "let go" is not to adjust everything to my liking but to live one day at a time and love myself in it.

To "let go' is to not regulate and criticize others but to become what I dream I can be.

To "let go" is to not regret the past but to live for the future.

To "let go" is to not focus on my mistakes but to learn the lessons and throw away the experiences.

To "let go" is to allow love to replace my fear.

Knowing Who You Really Are

One of the most interesting things that I learned during and after my divorce was learning who I was. I know it may sound silly, but before that time I would have emphatically said, "Of *course* I know who I am." But the truth of the matter was I did not have a freaking clue who I was. I had spent my entire life being who I thought I *should* be and who others *told me* to be.

In my training with Pia Mellody, she taught me how to determine my own reality by examining four essential elements of myself: my thinking reality, my feeling reality, by body reality, and my behavior reality. This was important because once I took the time to notice and determine the four elements of my reality, I could be legitimate with myself and with others without feeling shame. I could then agree to disagree with others and be okay with myself even if others were not okay with me.

Here is an explanation of how I did it.

Thinking Reality

The first part of my thinking reality that I wanted to examine were my religious beliefs. (I know this can be a sensitive subject, so let's proceed gently!) I had been raised in a fundamental Baptist church in a small West Texas town. On Sunday mornings, our church schedule was Sunday school at 9:30 and worship service at 11:00. In the afternoon and evening, we had choir practice at 5:00, training union at 6:00, and another worship service at 7:00. The doctrine that we were taught was extremely rigid and excluded those who believed differently. The minster would pound the pulpit and yell about the possibility of burning in hell for eternity if you did not publicly claim the doctrines as your truth.

I remember wondering how God could be so vicious and scary as to banish someone to eternity in a fiery furnace for using the brains he gave them.

At the end of the service, for those parishioners who wanted to dedicate their life to these beliefs, the preacher offered the opportunity to walk down the aisle in front of the congrega-tion. I think from age seven to twelve, just to make sure that my redemption bases were fully covered, I walked down to the front three times.

As an adult, I have a different set of spiritual beliefs that resonate in my soul as truths. I've discarded a lot of what I was taught as a child, and I feel really good about that.

I used this same process in evaluating what I believe about many big topics including politics, war, homosexuality, mar-riage, divorce, aging, and love, as well as things like food and fashion. I have learned to take what I like and leave the rest, and I have also given myself permission to change my beliefs if something no longer fits.

About two years into my single life, I stood before my closet one day looking at some of the clothes I had bought dur-ing the final year of my marriage. I was totally perplexed as to what I must have been thinking when I purchased these things. It was as if an alternate being had inhabited my body on the way to the mall. There was a pair of floral cropped pants, a sweater with a crocheted dog applique on the front, and a jacket with all sorts of dangling trinkets and fringe hanging off the sleeves. Even as I write this description, I cringe at the thought of prancing around Dallas in those hor-rific outfits. I realized I had bought those clothes because they were someone else's taste, not mine. That day I did a major closet clean out, and as I looked at each item in my collection, I asked myself one question: "Is this me?" If the answer was "no," it went straight into the Goodwill box.

Feeling Reality

As children in our family, we did not identify and talk about what we were feeling. No one had permission to feel angry with one another, and sadness was acceptable only if we did not cry too long or too loudly. I can remember my mom standing at the kitchen sink slamming pots and pans, fuming with anger and breathing heavily. It was obvious that she was very angry, but when my father asked her what was wrong, she replied, "NOTHING!" As my dad continued to pressure her into talking about her frustration, my mom's anger seemed to grow.

Finally, she broke into tears and admitted that she was angry because my dad, sister, and I did not get up after dinner and help her with the dishes. Although she did not ask for our help, she had a preconceived notion and we would know what she wanted without her asking. At that time, West Texas women were not taught to ask for what they wanted or needed. They were not given permission to express feelings in a healthy and appropriate way. Women who expressed anger were considered to be bitchy, whereas men had full-blown permission to yell, fight, and rant and rage. Crying was acceptable as long as it was not too dramatic.

Training with Pia Mellody opened my eyes to the necessity of learning how to identify my feelings, and she also stressed the importance of giving myself full permission to appropriately feel my feelings. Pia identified the eight basic feelings and their derivatives, which was a huge help for me. They are:

FEELINGS and their DERIVATIVES

1. **Anger—Resentment, Irritation, Frustration**
2. **Fear—Apprehensive, Overwhelmed, Threatened**
3. **Pain—Hurt, Pity, Sad, Lonely**
4. **Joy—Happy, Elated, Hopeful**
5. **Passion—Enthusiasm, Desire, Zest**
6. **Love—Affection, Tenderness, Compassion, Warmth**
7. **Shame—Embarrassed, Humble, Exposed**
8. **Guilt—Regretful, Contrite, Remorseful**

Later, in therapy, I was taught that feelings are not good or bad; they are simply emotions (energy in motion) that will dissipate as I feel them and allow them to pass through me. So how does a person feel their feelings? Here is my four-step process to feeling my feelings:

Step 1—Identify which feeling you are experiencing (see feeling chart above).

Step 2—Practice accepting that feeling. Ex: "Wow! I am feeling really angry." Acceptance does not mean that you like what you are feeling. It simply means that it is what it is.

Step 3—Shut your eyes, if possible, and breathe deeply for four breaths.

Step 4—On the inhale of your fifth breath, visualize the feeling(s) coming up from your body. On the exhale, visualize the feeling leaving your body as you blow it our into the air.

Because I learned that what I resist will persist, even my uncomfortable feelings are now welcomed friends that I can entertain for a while before letting them go. This one thing helps me enjoy my life more fully because I realized the more I feel my not-so-fun feelings, the more fully I get to experience the fun feelings like joy, passion, and love.

There are two other tools I use to help me manage my feelings. The first one is **H.A.L.T.** When I find myself feeling on edge or unsettled, I ask myself if I am **H**ungry, **A**ngry, **L**onely, or **T**ired. If the answer is yes to any of these, I halt (stop) what I am doing and do what I need to take care of my hunger, anger, loneliness, or tiredness.

The second option to dealing with feelings is the formula W_2T_2—**W**rite about it, **W**eep about it, **T**hink about it, **T**alk about it. All four of the actions will help to get you through whatever uncomfortable feelings you are experiencing.

Body Reality

Learning about my body reality was somewhat alarming. I realized that I often pushed myself excessively hard, even when I felt ill or when I was tired. I simply did not give myself permission to nurture my body during those times I needed tender, loving care. I also looked at my body as if I were looking through a microscope with the sole purpose of finding each and every flaw, pooch, or bit of cellulite. I would then walk away, feeling disgust and discontent because of what I found.

After having my first child I became obsessed with getting skinny. At 5'3" tall, I got down to 97 pounds by eating very little and exercising obsessively. My mother actually told me that one of her friends thought that I was terminally ill because I was so thin.

This was a terrible thing to do to myself. The human body is continually changing, and perfection is an illusion. Looking at myself through hypercritical eyes made body satisfaction and love for my body impossible to realize. As I write this, I am sixty-nine years old, and I like my body now more than I ever have. I no longer criticize my body, and I am healthy and eternally grateful to be alive and free from disease.

Behavior Reality

Looking at my behavior had a lot to do with understanding how it affected other people. I noticed that if I smiled at people, they smiled back and stood up straighter, and if I frowned at someone they tended to look away and slump. Because there is an exchange of energy when people look eye to eye, we can empower those with whom we come in contact. On the flip side, we can disempower others by the way we speak to or look at them. The fact that we influence change in the world one life at a time is a sobering realization for all of us.

To help you discover your reality, I suggest that you do this simple visualization exercise. Buy four different magazines: travel, food, home décor, and fashion. After you have the magazines, plan an uninterrupted time when you can sit somewhere lovely with soft music playing in the background. As you turn each page of the magazines ask yourself, "Is this me?" If the answer is yes, cut out the page and make a picture pile for each type of magazine. Once you have completed your four picture piles, look back through them and take out your favorites. Paste these on a poster board entitled "This Is Me," and upon completion, hang it somewhere you see it every day.

Get a Life

Creating a life for yourself away from a relationship can be exciting and extremely rewarding. Find something that stirs passion in you and visualize what it would feel like to follow that path. Get a job, go back to school, start a hobby, or find any other activity that can hold your interest. This will make you more interesting as well as more attractive to a person who also has a life. Men frequently tell me they are attracted to women who have an outside interest and are financially independent. They are looking for someone who is not needy, as a child is.

If you find yourself without a purpose or direction due to a divorce, death, or children leaving home, this is not an ending! It's the beginning of living life from the inside out rather than the outside in. You go from living for others to living for yourself.

When I got my divorce at age forty-two, I went to graduate school. I got a master's degree in counseling, and now I have a thriving private practice that is fulfilling and profitable. It was absolutely the best thing I could have possibly done. If I can do it, so can you!

Learn to Be Your Own Biggest Fan

My therapist told me one day that she had never met anyone more critical of themselves than me. Initially, I disagreed with her, but when she asked me to name ten things that I really liked about myself, and I could only come up with a grand total of five, I realized that she was right. When she asked me how I felt about this newfound truth, tears started streaming down my face. No wonder I had very little self-esteem or self-love. I would not want to spend time with someone who only had five things that I liked about them.

After that a-ha moment with my therapist, I was determined to find a way to learn how to like myself. I started by going on a daily "me walk" and coming up with an attribute of mine for every letter of the alphabet. The attributes could be physical, emotional, psychological, or behavioral. For the letter "A" I could say, "I really like my attitude." Then I would move on to the letter "B" and say, "I really like my blue eyes." I used each letter of the alphabet, except for the letter "X," which I substituted the syllable "ex."

I did this exercise for many years when I was feeling down on myself. I have often thought that this would be a wonderful family exercise while sitting around the dinner table. Self-approval never leads to arrogance. Arrogance is how people cover up their insecurities, whereas developing your self-awareness and approval is the way to eliminate insecurities.

Fix Your Picker

A key part of success in dating is being able to pick the right people to date. From a psychological perspective, the perfect time to do some work on your picking instinct is *before* getting into another relationship. Examining your family of origin issues and looking at your relationship history can break deep-rooted patterns of behavior that have proven to not work for you in the past.

For example, if you were given the role of emotionally or physically taking care of your parents or siblings, you may be attracted to men or women who need or want to be taken care of. People frequently duplicate both functional and dysfunctional patterns of behavior from their assigned roles and from watching the dynamics of their parents.

We also tend to pick people with some of the same dysfunctional behaviors that we have experienced in past relationships. It's like the people you date all wear the same coat. The fabric may look different, but the cut is the same. Maybe in the past you have picked people with alcohol abuse issues or other addictive behaviors such as work, sex, religion, codependency, or pornography. Even though these relationships are filled with pain and drama, you do it again and again as you tell yourself, "This time it will be different." As Albert Einstein said, the definition of insanity is doing the same thing repeatedly and expecting a different result.

Why on earth would you be willing to settle for a man with huge issues? You deserve better! Hiring a professional counselor or therapist can lead you into an understanding of why you continue to pick these people. Understanding the "why" is the beginning of healing. If you do not fix your picker, I guarantee that your picks will not change!

Make a List of Your Desires and Deal Breakers

Make a list of what you want in a relationship. Not what you think you *should* want or what other people have *told* you to want, but what you really, really, want. Be specific. Put anything and everything on this list, and do not judge yourself for what you want. I had twenty-six things on my list, and even though there were a few things that I could have lived without, my second husband has all twenty-six of them!

Make sure that your list is realistic. Recently, my five-year-old granddaughter, Mia, told me that she wanted a live kitten and a live unicorn for her birthday. Wanting a live kitten is possible but wanting a live unicorn is setting herself up for a big, fat letdown! Insisting that Mr. Marvelous is financially secure is definitely possible, but insisting that he's a billionaire is setting yourself up for a big, fat letdown and a lifetime membership in the Lonely Hearts Club.

This list gives you a format for visualizing Mr. Marvelous. Spend five minutes every morning when you awaken and every night before you go to bed reading your list out loud and picturing this man being in your life. At the end of the five-minute period, thank the Universe for bringing the right person into your life, and then get on with your day with joy. The focus here is on what *you* desire rather than making yourself desirable! Bobby Klein, one of my amazing spiritual teachers, says, "If you do not have a dream, how can you ever have a dream come true?"

The second list I want you to make is one of your absolute deal breakers. These are the things that if you see one or more of them in someone you date, the deal is off! They are non-negotiable because living with such behaviors will cost you your joy, your health, your spirit, and your self-confidence.

There should be no more than seven items on this list. I suggest that you place it on your bathroom mirror in case you need a friendly reminder. My deal breakers were: (1) infidelity; (2) active addiction of any kind; (3) *untreated* mental illness including depression, anxiety, and obsessive-compulsive disorder; (4) physical, verbal, emotional, psychological, or sexual abuse; and (5) an unwillingness to attend couples therapy if needed or wanted.

No matter what you may feel, do not make excuses to justify someone's unacceptable behavior. Deal breakers mean that the deal is *off.*

If infidelity is on your list, you will need to define what that looks like to you. Make the definitions specific and behavioral. For example, my definition of infidelity means kissing another woman, having sex with another woman (duh), having a secret friendship with another woman, and having a virtual sexual relationship with another woman. FYI… If you are currently dating someone who has a history of infidelity and he has not done serious therapy around this issue, bid Mr. Hanky-Panky Pants goodbye.

These two lists will keep you from turning into a chameleon, conforming to what other people want you to be or how other people want you to think. Be yourself unapologetically. This is *your* life, and you deserve a loving and joyful relationship that is right for *you.*

Section II:

The Dating Game

Kristan

"I was on a date with this really hot model. Well, it wasn't
really a date-date. We just ate dinner and saw a movie.
Then the plane landed."
—Dave Attell

*The first time I met with Kristan, she
was struggling to determine where she
wanted to go to college. Kristan was a
brilliant student, and after being accepted
into several top universities, she decided to
attend Harvard. It had been two years since
our last meeting, and I was looking forward
to hearing about her college experiences.*

*As Kristan entered my office, I was immediately
reminded of her poise and stunning beauty.
After taking a few minutes to discuss her love
for Harvard and her decision to major in
business, I asked what brought her into my
office that morning.*

*"Well," she said, "I'm really frustrated with
the whole dating thing. I've been on a ton of
dates and even kind of liked a few guys, but*

after seeing someone for a couple of months, I just do not see a future with any of them."

"So what happens after a couple of months of dating a guy?" I asked, "Do they do something that is on your deal-breaker list? Or do you not find them physically attractive?"

"There have been a couple of times when someone has done something on my deal-breaker list, like cheating," Kristan answered. "But for the most part, I just cannot find the perfect guy for me. When I realize that something is missing or we have a small conflict, I start to feel anxious and I want to run for the hills."

"Is this the only thing that triggers you to leave a relationship?" I asked.

"Not really," Kristan replied. "I also begin to feel a little suffocated, especially if someone tells me that they are really starting to like me and want me to date them exclusively. It is like I have a plastic bag tightly wrapped around my face. This feeling tends to get bigger and bigger, and if I try to hang in there, my anxiety starts to get out of control. The only thing that helps rid me of the suffocating feeling is to tell them that I do not want to see them any longer."

"So after you end the relationship, how do you feel?" I asked.

"I always feel a little bit guilty for hurting someone's feelings, but mainly I feel relief, like I can breathe again. What's wrong with me?"

"There's nothing wrong with you. What is happening is that your need for your own perfection is driving you to need perfection from a guy you like. Wanting high standards for both yourself and someone who could be your Mr. Marvelous is not a bad thing. But needing perfection from another human being is going to make it impossible to find a person with whom you want to spend your life. As human beings, we were all created perfectly imperfect, and learning to wrap your brain around this concept is going to be absolutely essential in order for you to be happy. Not only is it important for you give up the need for perfection in others but also time for you to exercise giving up need for perfection with yourself."

"Wow," said Kristan. "I see where it would be hard to 'be me' or 'be with me' if perfection is what I expect from myself and others."

"That's very true," I replied. "Now remember that we are not going to throw the baby out with the bathwater. Your desire for achievement, getting what you want in life, and finding someone with whom you are comfortable and compatible does not need to be eliminated. I just want you practice moderation in all

areas of your life. Remember that it is process and not an event, so be easy on yourself."

"Can I call you if I have trouble with this?" Kristan asked.

"Of course." I replied. "Call me anytime."

She did call, a few months later, to tell me she had just gotten engaged to Mr. Marvelous.

Chapter 4
Let the Games Begin!

No More Shame in Your Game

Let's say you've completed the arduous tasks of cleaning out your relationship closet. You have grieved the losses and dumped the contact stash of the ones who got away. You have put on your big-girl financial panties and learned to be comfortable in your own skin. To load on more metaphors (hey, why not!), now you're ready to cast your fishing hook out into the pool of possibilities. Even though this decision can feel daunting, I want you to remember that you now have a totally different relationship with yourself.

There is no more shame in your game.

You know who you are, and because you have made a list, you know what you want. From your list you are visualizing your future Mr. Marvelous twice a day and getting excited about the new possibilities. Also, because you made a list of your deal breakers, you know the specific things that you absolutely will not tolerate in your next relationship. Knowing that you will not stay in a relationship if a guy "acts the fool" takes some of the fear out of dating again. You can rest assured that you will have your own back, no matter what!

So, how do you go about getting out there? The first thing that I did when I was ready to date after my divorce was to *tell people I was ready*. I felt strange at first, like I should not have to be telling people. When someone asked me if I was dating, I always answered, "I'm dating, but not anyone specific right now." It was a weird feeling, but after a while I got used to it. I learned that it was okay to be vulnerable enough to promote myself. I went out on a lot of dates because I had committed to myself that I would say yes more than I would say no. Even though there were a lot of guys with whom I did not want to go on a second date, I met some very interesting people.

One day I was standing in the checkout line at my neighborhood grocery store when the man behind me said, "I noticed that you do not have on a wedding ring, and I was wondering if you're single or just mad at him." I laughed and told him that I was single. He then asked if I wanted to meet for a drink sometime, and I said sure. We chatted for a several minutes about kids and schools, and then I gave him my phone number. We ended up going out a few times, and even though it was not a love connection, it was great practice for me.

Prepare yourself for having pre-date nerves and for those first dates to be awkward. Remember that people love to talk about themselves, so ask a lot of questions. It's also a good idea to take a little time before your dates and think about potential topics that interest you and current events that are not controversial. If the conversation starts to lull, travel, hobbies, and children can easily be dead-zone fillers.

I encourage you to *not* ask about what happened in their failed marriage, and I also suggest that you do not trash your ex. Ripping your ex apart and acting like a victim will make you look like a bitter man-hater. Remember that because there was a time when you picked your ex, you had a part in the blundered relationship. You were there because of you.

The past is gone. Focus on the present and the future.

Do not allow the man whom you just met come to your house to pick you up. I always met a first date at a public location where there were other people around. Being in a public place provided security, and having my car gave me total flexibility to leave when I was ready to leave.

Online dating is another option that is extremely popular right now. It was just beginning when I was single, and I never used those services. Even though many people have had great success on dating websites, make sure that you are cautious. Some dating websites are known for being full of sex addicts, so do some investigation before signing up. And obey the number one rule of internet dating services: never give the guy your address and always meet in a public place.

Performing a criminal background check on the guy isn't a bad idea either. A statewide record check will cost you about twenty dollars. This type of report generally includes address history, age, misdemeanors, felonies, offense date, case number, arrest history, and offense description.

Don't get discouraged if it takes a while to get your dating sea legs! For most second-timers who have been married for years, the first few dates can be filled with anxiety. Be yourself, have some fun, and remember that the guy is probably just as nervous as you are.

Me

"My father always said, 'Be the kind they
marry, not the kind they date.'
So on our first date, I'd nag the guy for a new dishwasher."
—Kris McGaha

*Two years after my divorce I dated a guy
who lived in West Texas. As the president
of a very large company, his job was not only
to continue building the bank's assets but also
to carry on the tradition of being a pillar in the
community. His father and grandfather had
established a reputation of being extremely
"nice," which included flowering customers
with compliments, never voicing an opposing
viewpoint, and making sure that he always
had an ear-to-ear smile plastered on his face.
I must admit that his positivity was much
better than hanging out with Donny Downer,
but I had a nagging feeling that part of his
extreme optimism was a veneer.*

*One day we were in the elevator of a hotel
where Mr. Zip-pity-Do-Da stayed when
he was in Dallas. Before the elevator door*

closed, the manager of the hotel entered the elevator and my then-boyfriend said, "Hey, John, I see that you guys have laid new carpet throughout the hotel. It looks absolutely fantastic!"

After replying, with a resounding "Thank you," the manager exited the elevator, thrilled that his patrons would be amazed at his decorating talents.

Now let me tell you about that carpet. It was a combination of orange, brown, yellow, and tan fibers all mixed together. It literally looked like someone had thrown up on the carpet and no one was able to adequately clean all of the residue. I would have not even put that carpet in my garage! That is how ugly it was.

I looked at my boyfriend and asked, "Did you really liked the carpet?"

"No. I thought it was terrible."

"So why did you tell him that you thought it was fantastic?"

"I was just trying to be nice. I wanted John to be happy and feel good about himself. I have worked really hard to get special rates and privileges at this hotel, so a little schmoozing will help me get what I want."

After a moment of processing what I had just experienced, I said, "So when you tell me that I look fantastic, are you being honest with me or are you just trying to schmooze me like you did with John? FYI...I would prefer that you say nothing rather that saying something that you do not believe just to be nice."

From that point forward, I never really trusted what he said or did. He cheated, I got out of the relationship, and without any doubt, I dodged a bullet!

After stumbling through a handful of dates, you may have found someone who could have potential. This chapter is important because effective dating is not like fairy dust falling from heaven, landing on your head, and voilà, you get it right this time. Dating well is more about holding on to yourself, taking a deep breath, and doing things differently than you have ever done before.

I've divided the dating game into three stages, which are applicable to any new relationship: the marketing phase, the comfort zone, and the "here comes the bride" zone. Within each stage, I identify some very important techniques and principles, which if understood and utilized will prevent you from going too fast too soon and having your heart broken as the result.

Chapter 5
Navigating the Marketing Phase (1 to 4 Months)

The Marketing Phase

The marketing phase lasts one to six months. I call it the "marketing phase" because at the beginning of any new relationship, I will be marketing me and you will be marketing you. Honest marketing of oneself is not deceptive; it's just that you will primarily show your potential squeeze the best parts of yourself.

Can you imagine if on the first or second date, the woman said, "I would like to tell you a few things about myself. I am terribly moody in the morning and especially during my time of the month. I have on occasion thrown a few things in a fit of rage, but I have never sent anyone to the hospital. I will cry uncontrollably, spend an outrageous amount of money on shoes, and will lie about the cost of just about everything. I will eventually show you that I hate to cook and hate giving oral sex, and I am psycho about you hanging up your clothes immediately after you take them off. Oh, and by the way, make sure all of the hangers are facing in the same direction."

Then the man replies, "Good to know. There are also a few things about me of which you should be aware. No worries about your moodiness during your time of the month. I will keep a calendar of your cycle, and on those dates I will make sure to plan a sudden business trip that includes thirty-six holes of golf per day. I will never get up in the middle of the night to feed a newborn, and I will often work late, especially when the kids are very young. I want to have sex every night, or morning, and I will totally expect you to lose all your baby weight within sixty days after giving birth. I will continually watch sporting events (I include porn as being a sporting event) on the weekends and will rarely agree to watch a movie of your choice unless the movie is R or X because of extreme violence, massively bloody murder scenes, and total nudity. I will never give you my passwords to any of my devices, and I will drink beer with my buddies whenever I choose."

During this phase, you want to be honest but not necessarily discuss your every flaw or every mistake that you've ever made. As people date for a period of time, more is revealed, and there will be plenty of opportunities to get down and air your dirty laundry. If you *want* fun, then *be* fun, and remember that positivity is very attractive.

During the marketing phase, there's often a sense of overall euphoria. After just a handful of dates, you may start to think he's your Mr. Marvelous. If this stage is not well understood, you could run off to Las Vegas for a quick wedding believing that he's a gift from heaven, only to find out that the guy is a total sociopath or an unemployed deadbeat.

Red Flags

Rather than feeling love, both of you could become victims of a myriad of chemical combinations flooding your brains. The result is often a premature idea that this person is your everlasting love. There are some key warning signs, and if you recognize them and act accordingly, you could save yourself from an extended stay at Heartbreak Hotel.

The Price of "Nice"

"The Price of Nice" is one of my very favorite tools in learning to differentiate between being kind and being nice. If, like me, you were taught to be nice, no matter what others did or said, the following information has the potential to remove an ineffective vail of nicety that may have impeded your ability to live life legitimately.

Insufferable "nicety" (courteous, deferential, nonassertive, nonconfrontational, etc.) does not allow for real relationships that really count. In many ways "nice" is a cover for displaced aggression and hostility...at others and often at the self. When feelings and affect are not honored and allowed to emerge, these disowned and authentic feelings will eventually materialize in unhealthy and self-defeating ways (e.g., depression, headaches, sexual dysfunction, substance and process addictions, passive-aggressive behavior).

- "Nice" behavior tends to create an atmosphere such that others avoid giving him/her honest, genuine feedback. This blocks his/her growth.
- "Nice" behavior will ultimately be distrusted by others. It generates a sense of uncertainty and lack of safety in others. They can never be sure if they will be supported by the "nice guy" (or girl) in a crisis situation that requires any sort of an aggressive confrontation with others.
- "Nice" behavior stifles the growth of others. They avoid giving others genuine feedback, and they deprive others of a real person to assert against. This tends to force others in the relationship to turn their aggression against themselves. It also tends to generate guilt and depressed feelings in others who are intimately involved and dependent upon honesty in the relationship.
- Because of his/her chronic "niceness," others can never be certain if the relationship with a "nice" person could make it through conflict or an angry spontaneous confrontation. This greatly limits the potential extent of intimacy in the relationship, and when this occurs, others will adapt by being continuously on guard.

- "Nice" behavior is not reliable. Because the "nice" person is human, he/she may have an occasional outburst of rage, which will catch others off guard and they will be ill equipped to deal with the angry individual.
- Because the "nice" individual holds his aggression and frustration inside, he/she may experience psychological issues such as depression, anxiety, and alienation.
- A part of all relationships is conflict resolution. Acting "nice" instead of addressing issues severely impedes one's ability to create growth for the individuals in the relationship.
- The greatest benefits of emotional transparency are honesty, trust, respect, forgiveness, and an appreciation of others. The relationship will continue to grow as you rest assured knowing that even in your "not so nice" moments, you can count on yourself and your partner.[1]

"I Feel Like I've Known You For Years..."

If he tells you he feels like he's known you for years, don't be seduced by the idea that finally you have met someone who will really understand you. This person may feel like he's known you for years because there are things about you that are similar to someone he dated in the past (either functional

---

1   Adapted from G. Bach and H. Goldberg, Wellness Institute, *CreativeAggression: The Art of Assertive Living* (Garden City, NY: Anchor Press, 1974).

or dysfunctional), or maybe you have some of the same traits as his mom or sister. The only way he can understand you is by spending time with you. As you date for a period of time, the two of you will discuss your ideas, dreams, desires, and values. Time is the only way to know if you are like-minded enough to be compatible.

"We're Soulmates"

The same is true of the premature idea that the two of you are soulmates. As romantic as this concept may sound and as ideally as it has been depicted by Hollywood, I do not believe for a single second that your soulmate is wandering the world like a puzzle piece, destined to fatefully land on your life puzzle. I do believe, however, that people can *become* soulmates as they grow to fall in love and collaborate in building a healthy marriage. Terrence Real, one of my mentors, taught me that a good relationship is something you *do* rather than something you *have*. If you want to learn how to create a healthy relationship, read Terry's book *The New Rules of Marriage.* It is groundbreaking!

Let's Go Straight to the Sex!

Intensity without history, or too much too soon, is another red flag, warning that you have slipped into one of the two above fantasies. The idea that you are so in love that all you want to do is roll around in the sack is really more about lust than about love. The problem with first-date sex, or whenever you become sexual, is that once people start using their bottoms they tend to stop using their brains. As difficult as it may be, the longer you wait to become sexual, the more sensible you will be as far as evaluating whether this person is someone with whom you could build a life. Although sex can be mind-blowing, it will not be enough to turn a dysfunctional man into someone you would want to take home to meet Mama.

Indicators of a Toxic Relationship

There are several indicators of a relationship leaning toward being or becoming a toxic relationship. It can be really difficult to identify this at the beginning of relationship. You may tend to minimize certain behaviors because you so desperately want the relationship to work. Even though seeing one or two of these does not necessarily mean that this relationship is doomed to be toxic, it is worth keeping it in mind. If your gut tends to knot at the onset of some behaviors, I suggest that you drive the behavior by a friend or therapist to get their reaction:

1. Your boyfriend is critical of who you are, finds fault about what you do, and he wants you to change.
2. He frequently picks at you about your clothing, hairstyle, or makeup.
3. He criticizes your desire to be with your friends.
4. You feel as if your boyfriend has more power in the relationship.
5. He is controlling and jealous (needs you by his side, questions your whereabouts, does not want you to be by yourself).

6. You feel like you are losing your ability to practice self-care.
7. You have the desire and hope that your boyfriend will change.
8. You are constantly feeling insecure.
9. Your boyfriend never takes responsibility for his behavior.
10. He refuses to discuss an issue.
11. Your friends and family express concern about the relationship.
12. His words and behaviors are not congruent (absence of trust).
13. You do not feel free and easygoing when you are with him; you feel drained after being with him.
14. He offers what he calls constructive criticism like, "Should you have that extra piece of pizza?"
15. You do not feel like you can be yourself.
16. You do not have a positive feeling about the future.
17. He complains about your schedule.
18. He has a victim mentality—blaming others for their issues.
19. He is extremely competitive.
20. You are expected to do all of the work—planning, making reservations.
21. You find yourself making excuses for your partner's behavior.
22. You constantly feel insecure.

Tips for Success

Just as there are red flags, there are also things you can do to facilitate the development of a real, lasting relationship.

Be Yourself

As you enter into dating arena, I want to encourage you to be legitimate and honest so that your date has an opportunity to see the real you. Although it's normal to put your best food forward when getting to know someone, make sure that you are being kind rather than merely nice. Growing up in a West Texas household, I was taught to be nice at all times. That often translated into me saying yes when I wanted to say no, and no when I wanted to say yes, depending on what I thought the other person wanted me to say. As an adult, I realized that it is not unkind to say, "No, thank you." It is very unkind to say, "No, you jerk." Know the difference!

Being political and diplomatic are additional tools in developing the ability to agree to disagree. While your goal in discussing differences is not to dumb yourself down so the other person likes you, your goal should be to reveal what you believe while maintaining the integrity of the relationship. In other words, what is good for the goose is good for the gander. This is being political. Being diplomatic means that you are sensitive to where the other person stands on a topic. In diplomacy, the ultimate goal is to obtain a peaceful resolution. Terry Real taught me that if I "win," then the other person loses, and therefore the relationship loses. I can either win or be happy.

Beware of the Fantasy

In my opinion, the biggest mistake someone can make at the beginning of a possible budding love fest is to create a fantasy. The only way you can legitimately get a true picture of someone is to spend time with them. With enough time, most people will show you who they are. One of the things I tell my clients to do when they are liking someone new is rather than saying, "John is very kind and thoughtful," say, "John *appears* to be very kind and thoughtful." Making this one little change can help you keep your feet grounded in reality rather than creating a premature fairy-tale fantasy.

Don't base your reality about someone on whom they *tell* you they are. I know enough about the human brain that I could probably convince a new acquaintance that I was a brain surgeon. But until you see me operate, don't buy it!

If you start to see that you have made up a small fantasy, and the reality and the fantasy are different, then instead of changing the reality to match the fantasy, change the fantasy to match the reality. Busting up the fantasy is absolutely essential. Living in fantasy means focusing on the imagined potential rather than what you are experiencing with this person.

After my divorce, the first guy I went out with appeared to being very kind. He always complimented me on my appearance, took me to very nice restaurants, and would drop by to bring me unexpected flowers or treats. I initially thought that I had hit the jackpot right out of the chute, but after two months, he suddenly showed me a totally different side. As we were driving down an expressway in Dallas, another car cut in from of us, and we almost drove into oncoming traffic. My date laid on the horn, started screaming and cursing uncontrollably, floored the gas, and started chasing after the other driver. I was absolutely terrified! I had never been with anyone who had demonstrated such extreme road rage. He continued to rant and curse about what had happened, and after fifteen minutes I asked him to please take me home. Rage was one of the items on my deal-breaker list, so the next day I told him that I did not want to see him again. Being true to myself in that incident gave me a lot of confidence in knowing that I had achieved the ability and courage to have my own back, no matter what.

Physical or superficial attraction cannot be your only measuring stick. You have to give yourself time to see what is below the surface. Because a sociopath can fake it for months, time is your friend. With enough time, even the most deceptive person will show you who they are. Maya Angelou said, "When people show you who they are, believe them." This is extremely wise counsel. Thank you, Maya!

"Stay Behind the Desk"

Considering all of my tidbits of advice, "stay behind the desk" is probably my favorite and also the most important.

At the beginning of the dating process, you will probably be pretty good at asking yourself if a person you are dating could be right for you. You have looked at your wish list and continued to look for any deal breakers. You understand that you are basically interviewing people to see if there is someone who might get the job of being your forever person. So far, you are confident in evaluating the situation and the possibility of the light remaining green.

But after a few months of dating, when you start to think that you are really liking this other person, a strange phenomenon often happens. Rather than maintaining the position of an interviewer who asks yourself, "Is this person is right for me?" you may change into an interviewee and start asking yourself, "Am I right for this other person?" In other words, rather than staying behind the desk and sitting in the seat of personal power, you may move to the front of the desk and switch seats with the interviewee.

If you make that switch, you will begin to lose your sense of personal power in the relationship. The original confidence that you felt will dissipate into thin air and will be replaced with waves of insecurity. As the interviewee, you may agree to do things that you do not want to do, and you might start making excuses for unacceptable behavior from the other person.

If you have this experience, go back to chapters 2 and 3 and implement those practices that got you on the road to self-care and knowing how incredibly precious and valuable you are. Remind yourself frequently of how fortunate any guy would be to have you in his life. It is very important that you keep your eyes open for any signs that you are compromising what you want just to feel a sense of security. Picture yourself in that big black chair behind the desk, and get back to evaluating if this is the right person for the job of being your main squeeze.

Victim No More

You are responsible for your life and your past choices. As daunting as this may seem, once you stop believing that you're a victim, you can start to change your life. This realization will give you the ability to respond to everything that happens in your life even if you did not create the negative experience. I like to think of it as be being a tail on a dog. If I am blaming another person for something that caused me pain, I have hopped on the rear of that dog and they are wagging me around every time I relive my perceived victimization. That dog does not even know, or care, that I am attached to his rear, and yet there I stay until I choose to hop off.

Most women are very familiar with the characters of Cinderella, Sleeping Beauty, and Snow White. In each fairy tale, these poor young women are victims of wrongdoing and perceive themself as being powerless over their life of doom and gloom. Miraculously, however, Prince Charming sweeps onto the scene, rescues them from their fateful demise, and they live happily ever after.

In the real world, there are many divorced women who cling to the idea that a handsome man riding a horse of wealth will rescue them from their "woe is me" existence. If you are one of these women, you will remain stuck in your dream world and will become discouraged and depressed. You *can* and *must* rescue yourself. Remember, Prince Charming is dead…or in rehab!

But Mr. Marvelous is out there, waiting to meet you.

The Seduction Game

The seduction game is a very powerful force in the beginning stage of dating. Women tend to seduce with sex, and men tend to seduce with power and money. Because acting powerful, spending money, and having sex alters the brain chemistry, it is easy to start believing that you may have hit the motherlode with your new relationship. The highs that are experienced can be so intoxicating that you turn a blind eye to other factors that do not work for you. It is very easy to start building a fantasy before enough time has passed, as you envision being the leading lady in the life of your dreams. Remember that it takes up to six months to learn who someone really is.

As a woman, you know that mind-blowing sex can go a long way in getting a man to do things that you want him to do. For example, a man might not have ever thought about paying your rent for a month, but after you have spun a 360 on his you-know-what, he may agree to pay your rent for a year. Following that performance, he will perceive himself as being the world's greatest lover. Because he tells himself that it was as good for you as it was for him, he assumes that he will continue to have the same rapturous sexual experience every time he sees you.

The danger of this sort of seduction game is that both parties may have unrealistic expectations. These expectations can lead to disappointments, arguments, and broken hearts.

However, if you agree to specifically contract for certain things, like sex for rent, then that is totally your business. In that case, he's strictly your sugar daddy, you're his kept woman, and the seduction game of your relationship has been established.

Dating Is Risky Business

Be aware of becoming overly accommodating. This typically happens after you realize that you are beginning to be really interested in someone. Once your interest intensifies, you may find yourself having anxiety about the possibility of that person changing his mind about wanting to date you. Because there is always the possibility of getting hurt, you may try to ease the fear by not voicing your opinions. You may also find yourself starting to say yes when you want to say no, or making excuses for the guy not doing what he said he will do.

Here's an example. The guy you have been dating says, "I'll call you tomorrow," but tomorrow comes and he does not call all day. In order to mollify the fear of this guy being somewhat shady and the relationship not working, you tell yourself something like, "Oh well, I know he is busy, and I feel certain that he ran out of time." I mean, really? It takes a total of fifteen seconds to call someone and say, "I wanted to tell you that I am totally swamped at work and have a business dinner tonight. Therefore, I won't have time to talk until tomorrow morning. Sleep well."

When people tell you that they are going to do something and they have either changed their mind or can no longer do it, it is their responsibility to let you know. If words and behavior are not congruent, you will start to lose trust in that person and the stability of the relationship will suffer. Trust is the very foundation of a good relationship, and it cannot be compromised.

Another way you may overaccommodate is by acting as if you have no needs or wants. Because we all know that neediness is not attractive and that men abhor a woman who suffocates them with neediness, you can easily go to the opposite extreme and be needless and wantless. When this happens, you are probably telling yourself that Prince Charming will think that you are the greatest thing since sliced bread since you are so agreeable and allow him to run the show. Just so you know, being excessively self-sacrificing is just as pathological as extreme neediness.

The best way to moderate neediness versus self-sacrifice is to think in terms of these existing on a continuum. At the zero end you have total self-sacrifice, and at the 100 end you have extreme neediness. The adult emotional maturity level is found anywhere between 30 and 70. I call this the "cradle of moderation," because it's where you will experience the gentle rocking motion of practicing self-care and self-acceptance. At times you may feel more needy, while at other times you may feel more needless/wantless. Giving yourself permission to have both in moderation will allow you to maintain a sense of empowerment as the relationship is taking form.

Learn to Accept Kindness

A couple of years ago, Susie, a forty-five-year-old client, came into my office to discuss her marriage. I knew that after her first marriage she had been single for ten years before marrying for the second time. I was hopeful that her second marriage of two years was not in trouble. After a few minutes of catching up on how her daughters were doing, I asked how I could be of help to her. With tears in her eyes she answered, "I don't know if I can stay in my marriage. Every day seems to be the same. I'm getting extremely *bored*."

As I continued to ask questions to get to the bottom of her boredom, I had no reason to believe that Jim, her husband, had been anything but honest, dependable, and kind to her. Suddenly, it dawned on me what was happening to Susie. I gently said, "I think that rather than boredom, you are experiencing the *absence of chaos*. Because of living with alcoholism and abuse in your first marriage, you're not accustomed to ordinary peace and tranquility. If this rings true to you, then the realization of this will help you to build a tolerance for both the kindness and the calm."

Susie smiled and exclaimed, "Of course! That's exactly what's happening to me. I'm so relieved to know what it really is. I can do this!"

If you had previously dated or been married to Mr. Crazy and then started dating Mr. Marvelous, it may take time to adjust to the unfamiliar feelings of calm and kindness. As strange as it may seem, there are many women who find it difficult to accept kindness from a man. If you were raised in a home where there was addiction, fighting, and any form of physical, verbal, or sexual abuse, you probably developed a tolerance for the chaotic energy that accompanies those behaviors. You may have suffered from adverse childhood experiences that put your brain into a permanent "fight or flight" mode, and even learned to equate "violence" with "family." This is not your fault—it's a normal survival skill. Children in abusive families learn strategies for survival, but those same strategies can lead to depression, self-harm, and other problems.

Even if the behaviors are not as extreme as existed in your home or past relationships, it's important that you insist on being treated with kindness. Don't minimize unkind behaviors by saying something like, "I know he does not mean to raise his voice at me," or "He would have never hit me if I had not complained about his drinking."

DO NOT JUSTIFY SOMEONE'S ABUSE. ABUSE IS ABUSE, AND IT'S NEVER OK!

The Dos and Don'ts of Texting and Emailing

Our world is becoming a society of texting and emailing. Most people receive a steady stream of digital messages about appointments, deadlines, world news, weather notices, and political opinions. Because these advancements in technology have enhanced our ability to keep in touch with people and situations around the world, many people have shifted from voice communication to texting and emailing as their primary means of communicating.

The one place where emails and texts have become a detriment is in the dating game.

Really getting to know someone in the beginning of a relationship is dependent on *talking* with one another. Without hearing someone's voice, it's very easy to ascribe incorrect tone and meaning to a conversation. Let's take the word "whatever." If I say "whatever" with a smile and lightness of tone, you will conclude that I sincerely do not have a problem with the information you have just given me. On the other hand, if I say, "what*ever*" with a sharp, strong, sarcastic voice, you'll understand that I am not liking the information.

It's simply too easy to damage a relationship through an incorrect interpretation of a text or email.

I can clearly remember how much I enjoyed chatting on the phone with my husband in the beginning of our relationship. Unlike my West Texas drawl, Tom has a lovely, almost radio voice that always sounded kind and sophisticated. On the nights when we did not see each other, we would talk on the phone for up to an hour. Those conversations were so much fun and very influential in the development of our relationship. Please do not rob yourself and your relationship of this sort of enriching experience.

Other than writing someone a love letter, the one place where I think emails and texts are beneficial in a relationship is in the communication of logistics. If I'm going to be running late or need to make a change in plans, then a written message can be quick and easily understood.

Elizabeth

"Everyone says that looks don't matter, age doesn't matter,
money doesn't matter. But I never
met a girl yet who has fallen
in love with an old, ugly man who's broke."
—Rodney Dangerfield

After working with Elizabeth for six months during her divorce, it had been a year since I had seen her. She really struggled with the idea of her marriage ending, but her husband refused to get help for his alcoholism and infidelity. After doing some family-of-origin work and coming to realize that divorce was not sinful, she decided that for her own mental health she simply could not stay in the marriage. I was really looking forward to hearing about her new career and to see how she and the children were doing.

When Elizabeth walked into my office, I was reminded of how pretty she was; but even though she had a smile on her face, I could tell that something was troubling her. After some chitchat about the kids and her new

Pilates studio, I asked her what brought her into my office.

"Well," she said, "I have met someone, named Bert, who I really like and we have been dating for four months."

"That is terrific," I said. "So how is that going?"

"It went really well for the first three months," she said. "I mean, he came on really strong from the beginning, and he even told me that he could see us getting married. He called me first thing every morning and a couple of times during the day. We traveled together both alone and with all of our kids. Everyone gets along really well with one another, and he is very generous with his gift giving and always paying for everything."

All of a sudden I realized that Elizabeth had tears in her eyes. "So talk to me about why you are feeling sad." I said.

After sitting in silence for a couple of minutes while Elizabeth regained her composure, she responded. "Two days ago he sent me a text saying that he could not do this anymore. He said that he felt like it was too much too soon and he just needed to breathe. What is so weird about it all is that he was the one who was doing the 'moving so fast' thing. I mean he wanted to see me every night that I did

114

*not have the kids, and a week ago he talked
with me about adding on to his house so that
my two kids could have their own bedrooms
after we got married. Literally in less than a
week, he went from talking about marriage to
breaking up with me. I cannot for the life of
me figure out what I did to cause this switch
within such a short period of time."*

*"Honestly, Elizabeth," I said. "You did
nothing to cause this to happen. I call
these kinds of men or women 'Dance Away
Lovers.' A Dance Away Lover is also called
an avoidant. They can come on really strong
and then because of the emotional memory
of childhood enmeshment with a parent, they
get triggered and start to feel smothered."*

*"What does the enmeshment look like?" she
asked.*

*"The enmeshment is when a parent uses a
child as the source of fulfilling the parent's
emotional needs. The parent needs the
child to succeed, excel, and be happy so
that the parent can feel happy and proud.
Because it is never a child's job to make a
parent feel anything, the child easily gets
overwhelmed. The emotional memory of this
emotional abuse gets triggered in the dating
relationship, and only way they can get relief
is to leave the relationship. At first, they are
all in and go from zero to one hundred way
too fast. They do this because deep down*

they have a fear of abandonment. The fear of abandonment is the result of the child feeling afraid that the parent would leave if the child did not do everything the parent wanted and needed. There is no separateness between a parent and a child when the parent needs the child. Has Bert been married before?"

"Yes, three times."

"Well, Bert clearly has never done any work around this issue, and until he does, he will never be able to stay in a relationship. Remember that intensity without history is a big, fat red flag!"

Chapter 6
The Comfort Zone
(4 to 9 Months)

Beware of the Dance Away Lover

At this point in the game, you've been dating the same guy for four to six months, and so far, you have not seen anything that turns your stomach into a knot. The two of you have probably been having sex, and you're beginning to think there's a real possibility that he may be Mr. Marvelous. You've spent enough time with him that your worries and insecurities have subsided, and you're relatively comfortable that he is actually whom he has appeared to be.

I say "relatively comfortable" because occasionally around the six-month mark, a guy who has commitment issues will allow his wandering eyes to take control of his brain. If this is happening to him, as he fantasizes about being with more than one woman, he'll start ogling and flirting with others.

The starring role in his fantasy can either be someone new or someone from the past with whom he had a sexual relationship. As a result of his sexual memories and fantasies, he'll experience a very strong craving to dip back into that honey jar. He may also have anxiety as he wonders if he could spend the rest of his life with only one sexual partner. Without addressing the underlying love avoidant issues around his anxiety, he'll have an uncontrollable urge to run from his current relationship, thus becoming Mr. Dance Away.

When you're on the receiving end of this experience, you'll be left confused and in pain. You may feel defeated because you believed he was fully available and committed to you and your relationship. Looking back, you could have sensed that something had changed, but you denied your gut. He may not have called as often, and you may have started to feel him distancing from you. You might have also noticed him eyeing other women, but because you didn't want to be a nag or a jealous girlfriend, you told yourself to just get over it.

If you have had any fear of abandonment issues in the past, they'll probably be triggered again when this relationship crumbles. I strongly suggest that you make an appointment with your therapist so that you do not become depressed. Remember that the love avoidant and love addiction cycle stems from childhood wounds and experiences. It was not because you were not enough. It was because *he* was not capable of dealing with his dysfunctional stuff. Even though the reality has been a rude awakening, I promise that you dodged a bullet.

If you want to read more about love avoidance and love addition, Pia Mellody's book, *Facing Love Addiction*, is amazing and well worth reading.

Let's Get Down and Dirty and Have Some Fun

Once you enter the comfort zone of a relationship and you both have passed through any desire to run for the hills, a sense of peace and ease will enter into your relationship. You'll start to fully believe that the man you're seeing is legitimately the person whom you'll continue to experience.

As you reach this point in your relationship, I strongly suggest that you look intently at the list you made nearly a year ago, when you were preparing to date. It's important to re-evaluate if Mr. Marvelous still exhibits those characteristics. By calculating what percentage of your relationship desires are being met with this person, you will get a relatively clear picture of your future. You probably would not buy a car, a house, or even a handbag if it had less than 75 percent of what you wanted, so why on earth would you consider settling for less in a relationship?

The Four Forms of Intimacy: Into You I See, and Into Me You See

When you see that you are still getting a high enough percentage of your desires, not only will you start to feel more comfortable, but you'll also want to start talking about many things that you may have avoided until now. Even if you have briefly discussed topics like whether or not you want to get married again or how you visualize your future, you'll want to revisit these topics on a deeper level.

1. **Intellectual intimacy.** Do you want to have children, or more children if you already have some? Would you be willing to consider relocating to another city or country? What are each of your career goals, and do you plan on retiring at any particular age? You may also delve deeply into one another's political and religious beliefs, along with talking about values that are nonnegotiable. All of these discussions are a form of intellectual intimacy. They will not only be enlightening but also give more stability to your relationship.

2. **Physical intimacy** is about physical proximity (being in someone's personal space) or non-sexual touching. Examples of physical intimacy are shaking hands with someone, hugging someone without any intention of sexual desire or arousal, and a non-sexual kiss on the check. Physical intimacy can exist between roommates in college, some work environments, and family members.

3. **Sexual intimacy** between two people is touch with the primary purpose of arousal, including kissing, sexual hugging, fondling, ogling, or voyeurism. When in a significant other relationship, all of these forms are permissible as long as both partners are willing participants.

Forcing any form of sexual intimacy with a noncompliant individual is sexual abuse and is absolutely not acceptable, even if you are a couple. If at any time during a sexual encounter someone tells another to stop, the activity *must* stop. This holds true no matter how long a couple has been together.

4. **Emotional intimacy** between two people is having feelings, recognizing feelings, and talking about feelings. The eight basic feelings that all humans have are anger, fear, joy, sadness, guilt, shame, love, and lust. Even though we are all created with these eight feelings, many people were raised in a family system or exposed to other environments where the identification and expression of feelings were prohibited. Although most men have been given permission to feel anger, they have not been allowed or nurtured to identify or talk about feeling fear or sadness. Women, on the other hand, have been given permission to feel sadness, but they have not been allowed or nurtured to identify or talk about feeling anger. Men who talk about feeling fear or sadness have been labeled "sissies," and women who talk about feeling anger have been labeled "bitches."

Breaking the stereotypical stoicism regarding the identification and expression of feelings is essential in the development of a strong and viable emotionally intimate relationship. Trying to get someone who is walled off emotionally to talk about his or her feelings is like going to a hardware store and looking for a loaf of bread. Not matter how much you hunger

121

for the bread, it's just not there. Talking about feelings can be difficult at first because being vulnerable will leave you feeling exposed.

Just so you know, however, an emotionally intimate relationship with you partner will not only provide you both with a feeling of safety but also supercharge your sexual relationship. Sounds good, huh?

Boundaries: Separateness Versus Enmeshment

Separateness is the practice of boundaries. Implementing a healthy boundary system will keep you from becoming enmeshed with other people. The saying, "If Mama ain't happy, ain't nobody happy," is the essence of enmeshment. Everyone around the unhappy Mama takes on Mama's burdens: her sadness, fear, guilt, or shame. As you implement a boundary system, you'll be able to realize that another person's experiences, thoughts, feelings, behaviors, and values are not your own. This doesn't mean that you do not have compassion for the person in their unhappiness. The word *compassion* means "with love." You can have compassion for them and love them without losing yourself to their experience. You can watch what they're feeling, for example, without assimilating their feelings as your own.

After my youngest daughter went away to college, she called me one morning in tears. She told me she was very homesick. I talked with her for a little while, and then we hung up the phone to go about our days.

For the entire day I felt very sad, wishing that I could do something to "fix" her melancholy. In the early evening, I called her back to see how she was feeling. She answered the telephone sounding happy and excited. When I asked her how her day had been, she answered, "Great!" She said that she and one of her friends had seen something funny shortly after we had spoken, which had changed her mood from sadness to joy.

I was happy for her—and then I realized I had literally sucked in her sadness all the way from Kansas to Dallas! Rather than having compassion for her and leaving it at that, I had felt her sadness all day long. I had lost myself, my joy, in what I perceived as being her emotional reality.

When other people are experiencing negativity, imagine yourself in a jelly jar. Watch them in their experiences without taking in their negativity. Ask yourself, "Is this what I am feeling? Is this what I am thinking?" If it is not yours, then do not let it in. Allow their experiences and feelings to bounce off your jelly jar and then float away. It is not that you don't care; of course you care when people are experiencing something that causes them to feel sadness, fear, or pain. But you need to realize that it's not your experience. It's not yours to "fix."

Perceiving that you need to fix someone is emotional caretaking, and that is simply no longer your duty. You are really needing and wanting them to feel differently so that you can feel differently. It's no one's job to make you feel anything. That's you needing to control them. When you stop trying to make everyone happy, you are allowing others the dignity of their own experiences. You stop playing God. Their reality is not about you, although it may affect you and your experience. It is really none of your business. It is not on your side of the street. You can have compassion for them without sucking in their stuff.

A boundary system also includes containing your own stuff so that others do not take it in and try to fix you. As you practice keeping yourself from trying to change others, you'll realize that it's not the duty of other people to take on your experiences and make you better. You can tell others that it's not their job to take care of you, thus releasing them from trying to accomplish an impossible task. In her book *Facing Codependence*, Pia Mellody does a wonderful job of explaining the details of boundaries. She taught me all that I know about boundaries, and for that I am eternally grateful.

The Warning Signs of Abuse

Even though we briefly touched on abuse in chapter 5, I want to define the different types of abuse and the behaviors associated with abuse. If you were raised in a family system that exhibited abusive behaviors, you may tend to tolerate abuse from others or exhibit abusive behaviors yourself. My goal is for you to eliminate *any* tolerance for abusive behavior in your relationship.

Verbal Abuse

Verbal abuse includes:

* **Name calling.** Some forms of verbal abuse are more overtly abusive than others. It is easy for most people to see that calling someone a "bitch" is abusive, but you may not realize that being called "stupid," "worthless," "a sissy," "a crybaby," or "a brat" are abusive as well.

* **Yelling and screaming.** If anyone yells or screams at you (or anyone else in front of you), it is abusive. It does not matter if it is your partner, boss, friend, another family member, or any other individual. Yelling and screaming should not be allowed in any home, under any circumstance. We tend to teach children that they should tolerate yelling from adults out of respect for the adults. I think this is absolutely ludicrous.

* **Not responding to or ignoring someone.** Ignoring or not speaking to someone out of frustration, hurt, or as a form of punishment may not appear to be abusive, but it is considered to be covert verbal abuse and is extremely damaging to any relationship. It is a form of emotional abandonment and makes the ignored person feel anxious and unsafe.

If you are feeling very angry and are afraid that you might lose your temper and yell, then you should say something like, "I am feeling angry right now, so I am going to be quiet for a bit so that I can breathe through this anger. I will talk with you about this in half an hour. These are my feelings, and it is my job to deal with them."

* **Sarcasm and teasing that is intended to mock or ridicule.** *Sarcasm* comes from the Greek word *sarca-zo*, which means "to tear the flesh." Like other forms of verbal abuse, sarcasm can be either overt or covert. Overt sarcasm would include a cutting remark or spiteful innuendo, while a scornful sneer would be considered covert sarcasm. You may be saying to yourself, "I am just teasing when I use sarcasm." Even if that's true, it's virtually impossible for the person on the receiving end of the sarcastic remark to differentiate a harmless tease from a putdown.

My father was raised on a ranch in Texas and was one of seven children—six boys and one girl. He was the only one of the children who attended college as an adult, and he continued to live away from his place of birth. When I was a little girl, my family would visit my father's family five or six times a year. I loved visiting my grandmother and playing with my cousins (there were nineteen of us), but I absolutely hated the times when all my uncles were around. They would tease me mercilessly, which resulted in me feeling terribly embarrassed and bursting into tears. My reaction to their teasing only spurred them on, as they called me "crybaby" and told me I was too "thin skinned."

I remember one incident in particular when my sister chased me with a firecracker. I was probably five years old and I was terrified. I started crying and screaming, and my uncles thought my response was hilarious. As I listened to them mock my crying and call me a crybaby, I desperately looked around for my father to rescue me. My father simply stood in the circle with his brothers and chuckled. Although I now understand that their intentions were not to shame me, the impact of their behavior was profoundly shaming. As I am writing this story, my stomach tightens, and I feel angry and sad that no one intervened on behalf of that precious little girl.

Because I was raised around adults who were masters at sarcasm, I, too, learned to be sarcastic. One morning after Tom and I had been married for several months, I went into the kitchen and saw that Tom had not washed all of his Grape-Nuts cereal down the sink after rinsing his bowl. I looked at him and sarcastically said, "I was just wondering if you were saving these Grape-Nuts for your midmorning snack, or you were expecting me to clean your breakfast residue for you?"

Tom replied, "That is sarcasm, and I do not like it one bit. Please do not talk to me like that ever again. If you had simply asked me to clean the sink, I would have happily done so."

I meekly apologized and made a promise to him, and to myself, that I would not use sarcasm ever again. Although it took me a while to practice putting my tongue between my teeth as a reminder to not verbalize my sarcastic remark, I can honestly say that I have kept my promise.

Physical Abuse

Physical abuse includes:

* Any type of forced physical contact
* Hitting any part of the body
* Face slapping
* Shaking
* Hair pulling
* Tickling into hysteria
* Pinching
* Allowing a child to witness or hear the physical abuse of another child or adult. Because children have not learned to differentiate themselves from others, witnessing or hearing the abuse of a parent or sibling will be internalized by the child as if it were happening to them.
* Ignoring or abandoning anyone who is incapacitated, including an elder.

I cannot resist the urge to include a note about spanking children. Spanking can seem to be the easiest way to discipline and has been called the "lazy man's tool for parenting." Although you and your parents may have believed that spanking was the only way to get a child to stop a particular behavior, history has shown that *it does not work*. Our prisons are full of people who were spanked and disciplined using various forms of physical punishment. It simply does not work. Most adults rightly tell children at a very early age that it is not okay to hit other people, and they may spank their children with an air of self-justification. Do you see how incongruent this is? How can it possibly be acceptable for a parent or anyone else to hit a child?

Most parents who use forms of physical punishment do so from a place of intense anger. The parents transfer their own anger or rage onto the body of their child. The child then internalizes the rage and will act out toward himself or others. If a child can be so "bad" as to cause his parents this amount of angst, he will question how he can possibly have any internal value. I strongly advise my clients *not* to spank their children.

Sexual Abuse

(Adapted from Pia Mellody)

Sexual abuse includes:

* Touching a person sexually without his or her permission
* Not negotiating when, where, and how to engage in sexual activity
* Demanding unsafe sexual practices
* Leaving pornography where others who do not wish to or should not see it may see it
* Exposing oneself to others without their consent

* Staring at or looking at another person lustily (voyeurism) without her permission
* Exposing visually and/or auditorily others to your sexual activities without their consent

Many forms of sexual abuse are serious criminal offenses, which can land the offender in prison and then force them to register as a sex offender. If you have the urge to commit any type of sexual abuse, get professional counseling immediately.

Emotional Abuse

(Adapted from The University of New Hampshire Sexual Harassment and Rape Prevention Program)

The emotional abuser:

* Calls you names, insults you or continually criticizes you
* Humiliates you in public
* Displays frequent jealousy or possessiveness
* Tries to isolate you from family or friends
* Looks at your texts, emails, or phone records without your permission
* Goes through your personal items such as wallet, handbag, backpack, or briefcase without your permission
* Monitors whom you call, whom you spend time with, and where you go

* Frequently blames you for their relationship problems
* Defines your role and attempts to keep you from working outside of the home
* Controls your finances and refuses your access to shared money
* Withholds affection as a form of punishment
* Threatens to reveal confidential information or anything that you want to keep private
* Threatens to commit suicide to prevent you from leaving the relationship
* Uses threats of hurting your family, you, or your pets as a means of control

Sexual Fantasies and Sexual History

Because most couples are having sex by this time in the relationship, it's extremely important for couples to be transparent regarding how they want their sex life to look. I suggest that people discuss not only the specifics of what they enjoy in real life but also what they fantasize about. I say, "If you had a magic wand and you could create the sex life of your dreams, what would that look like? Would you have sex twice a week or twice a day? Would you have a threesome with another woman or man? Would oral sex be important, and would it be a deal breaker if your partner does not want to give it or receive it? Would anal sex be a part of your fantasy (yes, there are a lot of heterosexual men who like it)? Would you like to participate in a group trip or event with swingers? Would you like to have other people watch you having sex? Would you like to watch pornography with your partner?"

There are as many different flavors of sexual desires as Baskin-Robbins has flavors of ice cream!

Knowing what your partner's values are regarding sex will prevent you from being appalled or blindsided further down the road. The key with sexual transparency is that each of you are able to *listen without judgment*. Even if you hear that your boyfriend might enjoy something that you would never do in a million years, it's imperative that you tell him the truth. For example, you could say, "I hear and understand that you might enjoy a threesome with another woman involved, but I need for you to know that I do not think that I would ever be willing to participate in that with you." You have given him information that will allow hm to make a decision about continuing the relationship. As scary as that may seem, being honest is being true to yourself. If someone leaves the relationship because of a different value, then the fairy tale would not have had a happy ending after all.

As far as sexual history is concerned, I absolutely do *not* believe that you should ever share the quantity or quality of your previous sexual partners. Even if bragging about past sexual conquests with your friends has made you feel like you were God's gift to men or God's gift to women, revealing information about past sexual partners and past sexual experiences to your romantic partner makes you look like scumbag. Keep it to yourself!

Section III:

I Think This Is My "Boo"

Sherry

"My boyfriend and I broke up. He wanted to
get married and I didn't want him to."
—Rita Rudner

*I was really looking forward to seeing
Sherry again. Sherry was a very successful
fashion designer and it had been two years
since our last appointment. At that time,
her previous boyfriend was transferred to
another city, and she was devastated that he
did not want to marry her and take her with
him. I was really curious to find out how she
was doing.*

*As she walked into my office, I was reminded
of how poised and beautiful she was, and I
was glad to see that she was smiling from ear
to ear. I felt pretty confident that Sherry had
some good news to talk about.*

*"Hi, Sherry!" I said as I got out of my chair
to give her a big hug. "I am so glad to see
you! Your glowing smile tells me that you are
in a really good place today, is that true?"*

"Yes, I am in a really good place," Sherry answered. *"My business is amazing, and my love life is better than I have ever known."*

"I am so happy for you," I said. *"You deserve all of the wonderful things that life has to offer. I would love to hear about all of the good things happening in your life, but I imagine that you did not make an appointment just to discuss how great you are doing. So tell me what you want to talk about."*

"Well," she said, *"I have met someone that I am crazy about. His name is Benjamin, and he is thirty-five years old, which is two years older than me. He's a successful investment banker, never been married, and truly one of the kindest guys I have ever met. He grew up in Mississippi, so he has some of those really great Southern manners, and his family is lovely. My mom has met them, and she agrees with me that he and his family would be a wonderful addition to our family. Since my dad passed away when I was fifteen, Benjamin's father told me that he would be honored to be my surrogate dad. I thought that was about one of the kindness things I have ever heard."*

"I agree," I said. *"How long have you guys been seeing one another?"*

"We started dating ten months ago, and I'm having some anxiety about whether or not

this relationship is going to last. We have talked about getting married, but he has not proposed as of now. There is nothing about him that I would say causes me concern, and even though there are no 'red flags,' I am definitely feeling some pretty strong anxiety almost every day. I cannot figure out why on earth I would be feeling anxious about Benjamin. I mean, I totally trust him, and he always does what he says he is going to do. What is wrong with me?"

"I'm pretty sure that I know what is happening with you."

"Great!" she responded. "Please fill me in, and please help me understand why I am so anxious. Am I just crazy?"

"No you are not crazy," I replied. "But you are human, and I truly believe that you are experiencing some fear of abandonment as the result of your father's premature death and the sadness related to the out-of-nowhere breakup of your last relationship. Our bodies store some powerful emotional memories, and then when an external event happens, we oftentimes will relive past repressed emotions and attribute them to our current day events. I think you are 'waiting for the shoe to drop,' expecting Benjamin to go away like your father dying and your last boyfriend leaving. Not only do I have some really good tips for you and Benjamin in evaluating your

relationship but also some great techniques to help you heal the wounds from the past. These techniques will stop you from reliving the pain that has nothing to do with the present or the future. Let's get started."

Chapter 7
Here Comes the Bride
(9 to 12 months)

Is This the Real Deal?

At this point, you're probably spending more time visualizing how your life will look being married to the guy whom you've been dating for the last nine to twelve months. Before shopping for your wedding dress, I hope that you have had a discussion around whether you both have the desire to get married at some point in the relatively near future. Initiating this conversation can be somewhat scary, for fear that one of you might hear the other say, "I do not know if I ever want to get married."

More men than women think that they do not need or want to get married, especially if the woman is willing to continue to be sexual without marriage. As archaic as it may seem, the old saying, "Why buy the cow if you can have the milk for free" still rolls around in the brain of many men, especially if they have been married before and already have children. If being married is what you really want, then you need to honest with Mr. Marvelous and let him know that you will not continue to date him forever. This is not coercing him into doing something that he does not want to do. Rather, it is telling him that you know what you want, and you are confident in your ability to find a man who shares your value around marriage.

Relationship Evaluation

In addition to your deal breakers, there are a few other questions I encourage you to journal about. Sit down with a cup of coffee or a glass of wine, and after taking the time to seriously think about each question, write down your answers. This will give you a ton of clarity as to the benefits or drawbacks of your relationship. If you discover a couple of issues that are of concern to you, it does not mean that you should leave the relationship. It may simply mean that the two of you have some areas that need a little work. Chatting with a therapist can provide some guidance in the areas of your concerns.

- What is it about this relationship that makes me feel so happy? How does this fit into my value system?
- How does this relationship effect my self-esteem? Do I feel more or less confident after being with this person?
- Do I feel anxious, depressed, or worried in this relationship? Do I feel this person is honest and trustworthy?

- Does this relationship have any sort of negative impact on my sleep or my health?
- Does this person encourage my career or demand that my work take a back seat to the relationship?
- Does this relationship encourage a broad or narrow outlook on life, friendships, values, or interest?
- Is this relationship primarily peaceful, volatile, or chaotic? If volatile or chaotic, what behaviors are exhibited?

As you look at your answers, ask yourself if you would encourage a relative or close friend to remain in the relationship or leave it.

As you are evaluating whether your relationship has a strong potential for the long haul, another tool to keep in mind is found in Aaron Beck's book, *Love Is Never Enough*. The book lists five things necessary in a healthy sexual relationship. These things also pertain to other healthy relationships excluding #2. They are:[2]

1. Trust—This happens when people's words and behaviors are congruent.
2. Fidelity—This is sexual faithfulness.
3. Loyalty—When your partner is in conflict, you do not take the other person's side. This may mean that you sometimes must remain neutral. For example, a parent with two adult children.

---

2   Aaron T. Beck, MD, *Love Is Never Enough* (New York: Harper Perennial, 1988).

4. Commitment—A promise made to one another to work through conflicts.
5. Compromise—This is a willingness to negotiate.

After you have completed these two most recent evaluations, you will either feel reassured that this person is someone good for you or you will have a nagging, uneasy feeling in your gut that something is simply not right. Because you have spent nearly a year developing a relationship, it would be easy for you to deny your doubts by rationalizing, justifying, and making excuses for why this gut feeling is incorrect. Please do not delude yourself into thinking that this person is going to change. *What you see today is what you will get in the future.* I promise that a lifetime of living with someone who is unfaithful, untrustworthy, disloyal, or not collaborative will be far more painful than grieving the loss of your fantasy. Have your own back and walk away. I know that you can do it, and I know that *you will survive!*

Money, Money, Money

A discussion about money can be uncomfortable and trigger many issues for a budding romance. Facing this topic head-on takes courage along with a willingness to be vulnerable. For example, if you tend to spend more than you make or have a substantial debt looming over you, you may be very hesitant to come clean about your money woes. Your fear is that Mr. Marvelous will run for the hills or disappear in the dead of night once he knows the truth about your spending habits. As difficult as it may be, it is essential that honesty prevails. Because we have already established the fact that it's *no one's job to rescue you financially*, being honest is the only way to go.

Whether or not you have been married before, it is important that are you aware of the financial situation of the guy who appears to be Mr. Marvelous. In 2011, Pamela Vip, a senior financial editor for the *Dallas Morning News*, interviewed Tom and I for an article regarding financial issues when people are heading into a first or second marriage. I stressed to Pamela that it's extremely important that before you get married, you each have full disclosure financially. This means how much you have in savings, how much you have in investments, and how much debt you have. This will ensure that each party is fully aware of where their partner is financially. Along with both parties viewing each other's credit report, I also suggest to my clients that they view each other's past five years of income tax returns.

Nine months into our relationship, Tom and I had several discussions about each of our individual financial statuses. It was a big relief to know that we both had the same basic value system around money. I also hired an attorney to do a background check, because I wanted to be sure that he had paid his income taxes and had no criminal history. Fortunately, Tom was clean as a whistle!

It's Not Always Roses: The Rules for Arguing

When two people spend a lot of time together, it is inevitable that there will be an occasional disagreement or argument. After dating someone for several months, some personal characteristics that you originally thought were endearing may become annoying. Also, at this stage of the game it's common for couples to find themselves wanting some time alone or more time to hang out with their individual friends. If Mr. Marvelous is not feeling the same way at the same time, he may feel hurt, angry, or afraid that the differences may mean that the relationship is in trouble. In other words, the once smooth ride may hit some bumps.

Even though conflict is very normal and very predictable, there are some fight rules that will help you weather the storm. Remember that your goal is to resolve the conflict while preserving the integrity of the relationship. If one person in the relationship "wins" the argument and the other person "loses," then the relationship loses. Couples who know how to resolve conflict by finding a solution often come out of an argument stronger than before.

Here are the basic guidelines for resolving conflict:

- Cooperatively agree to a time and place to talk before launching into the specifics of an issue. By setting a time and place and identifying the topic of discussion, both parties have the opportunity to think about the topic before the agreed discussion time. If one person has as issue, the other person cannot refuse to talk about it.

• State your issue by using positive "I" statements: "I want, I feel, I think..." If you are the listener, make sure to listen attentively. Turn off the television or radio, turn off your cell phones and Siri, and look at one another when listening. Avoid any negative body language, rolling of eyes, or passive-aggressive sighing. This is not the opportunity to revisit any old, unresolved issues.

• Ask for what will make you happy as opposed to demanding something from your partner. (The difference is subtle but very important!) A demand that your partner do something will typically trigger resistance, and it puts you in a parental position. You are not the boss of your partner, and no one will want to be sexual with someone who acts like a parent.

• Don't use absolutes such as "you always" or "you never." This is a provocative form of escalation and is most likely factually absurd. If you say, "You *never* bring me flowers!" your partner is likely to angrily respond, "What did I bring last week? Since when are roses not considered flowers?"

• Do not pull out a laundry list of unrelated gripes. This is called "mission creep" and is another form of provocative escalation. Only discuss one issue at a time.

- It's okay to complain about someone's behavior, but it's *never* okay to complain about someone's personhood.
- If your argument is a matter of opinion, then you may ultimately need to simply agree to disagree. If your argument is about something factual, then make sure you have the actual facts.
- Avoid ascribing intention to another person's behavior. You cannot know someone's intention without them telling you.
- Keep your discussion to the matter at hand rather than digging up unresolved issues of the past. Again, this is unwarranted escalation.
- Rather than preach a sermon about your concern, verbalize your complaint, and then allow the other person to respond.
- Make sure that you respond to the person's statements or answer the person's questions before bringing up a different issue.
- ABSOLUTELY NO NAME CALLING. Calling another person a derogatory name is verbal abuse and is never okay.
- Do not assume that you know what another person is thinking or their motivation for a particular behavior. Never try to tell them what they're thinking.
- There is no place for emotional blackmail in an argument. "If you wanted me to be happy you would…" or "If you loved me you would…" are "gotcha" questions that will only infuriate your partner.

- And finally (drum roll please…), leave his parents out of it! His mommy is not in the room, he is. Unless the conflict specifically revolves around an issue involving his parents, such as the behavior of Drunk Dad at the holiday party, then parents are off-limits.

As you argue, try to come up with alternative solutions for a particular issue. Accept the differences of others and remember that "different" does not mean "bad." Remember that your ideas are not the only answer or always the best answer.

Always keep in mind that the main goal of conflict resolution is to preserve your relationship. Work together to find a mutually agreeable solution. If that is not your goal, then I strongly suggest that you move on down that cafeteria line of men (or women).

Above all, while you're arguing, always be on the lookout for those subtle signs that he wants to de-escalate and resolve the problem. Sometimes silence is a sign that he wants to get back on the right track, or a simple nod of the head as you make a point. There's an old saying that goes, "No woman ever shot her husband while he was washing the dishes." Very true!

I love the following quote by Hugh Prather: "'You're wrong' means 'I don't understand you.' I'm not seeing what you're seeing… But there is nothing wrong with you… You are simply not me, and that's not wrong."

Claire

"Never laugh at your wife's choices. You are one of them."
—Anonymous

The first time I met with Claire she was a senior at Southern Methodist University and was struggling to decide which medical school she should attend after graduating. Claire had been accepted to three different medical schools, and the decision process for her was extremely stressful. At that time, I had suggested that she make a pros and cons list for each of her three options and then visualize herself attending each of the schools. I told her that her gut would then give her direction as to what the best choice would be. I was looking forward to seeing Claire again and hearing about how her first year of medical school was going.

As Claire entered my office, I could tell that she had been crying.

"Hi Claire," I said. "I am so happy to see you again. I could tell by your text message

I received yesterday that something pretty urgent had developed, and I am really glad that I was able to work you into my schedule. So tell me what is going on."

"Well, first of all, medical school is going great," said Claire. "I am really glad that I decided to attend UT Southwestern Medical School instead of my other options. Even though school is really difficult, I think that staying in Dallas was beneficial because of the familiarity. At least, I have not had to figure out an entirely new city. You were right about me being able to trust my gut after visualizing the pros and cons of each school."

"I am so glad that worked for you and that you are happy with your decision," I responded. "So what do you need help with today? It looks like you have been crying. Are you sad about something?'

"I've been crying and I'm really sad," answered Claire with tears welling in her eyes.

"Talk to me about what is making you sad," I said.

"Okay. I have been dating another medical student for about three months, and I really like him a lot. His name is Anthony and he's from New York City. We are in the same class, which is really helpful,

because we can study together, and we both understand the incredible pressure of being a second-year medical student. Anthony is Italian and is from a family of six kids. He is incredibly intelligent and also really funny. Our sex life was really great in the beginning, but lately Anthony has been too tired for sex at night and sometimes even on the weekends. Right now sex is pretty infrequent. I have never liked anyone as much as I like Anthony, and I really think that I am in love with him."

"Do you guys say, 'I love you' to each other?" I asked.

"Not yet, but I think that we will before long."

"Well, all of that sounds pretty good. So what is the issue that is creating this sadness?"

Claire looked down at the tissue in her hands, and as the tears started, she took a deep breath and began to explain.

"Two nights ago as we were going to bed, I noticed that Anthony put his phone underneath his pillow. When I asked him about it, he said that he put it there in case he got a call from the hospital. He said that he did not want to disturb my sleep. He gave me a quick kiss on the forehead, told me 'goodnight,' and then rolled over with his back to me. He had never put his phone under his pillow before, and I

thought it was very strange. I had a terrible feeling in my gut that something was up.

"I barely slept at all, and the next morning I told Anthony that I wanted to look at his phone. He told me that he did not have time for all of this and he got in the shower. Because he left his phone on the kitchen table, I picked it up to look at his messages and phone calls. When I unsuccessfully tried to log in to his phone, his code no longer worked. I then realized that he had change his passcode. When I asked him for his new code, he said that he no longer wanted me to have access to his phone. I started crying and then sent you a text."

"Claire," I asked, "what are you telling yourself about all of this, and what is your gut telling you about this?"

"Well, I tell myself that Anthony is right and that I should not have access to his email and phone passcodes. But then my gut tells me that he is hiding something from me and that there could be another woman in his life."

"Do you remember the activity that I had you do when you were trying to determine which medical school to attend?" I asked.

"Yes," Claire answered. "You had me write down the facts of the situation, pros and cons, and then to trust my gut."

"Well," I said. "I want you to do the same activity again regarding your relationship with Anthony. Then I want you to trust your gut and remember that your gut will lead you."

Chapter 8
The Nitty Gritty

The Nitty

A Background Check...Really?

On occasion, I will have a client who is seriously dating a man who has no history with the woman's family, friends, or acquaintances. In that scenario, the woman's only source of information about the man's past is what he has disclosed to her. If that is troublesome to the woman, I suggest that the woman hire an attorney to run a background check on her potential Mr. Marvelous. This inquiry would provide information on bankruptcy, arrest, and any other legal issues from the past.

Social Media

I believe that both people in a relationship should have access to passwords for phones and computers for the sole purpose of feeling confident that no one is being unfaithful. Even though they each have access to listen to messages and read emails and texts, I do *not* think it is okay to look through someone's phone or computer without their permission. I also believe that people who never leave their phone on the countertop or in another room, where their partner can see it, are setting themselves up for suspicion.

With the availability of Facebook, Snapchat, dating apps, and Instagram, it is very easy for individuals to keep in touch with ex-partners and/or create online pornographic relationships. In my opinion, once a couple determines that their relationship is exclusive there is no room for either of the aforementioned activities. Make sure that you bring to your partner's attention anything that is causing you concern. Allowing a sore subject to fester will often create a monstrous, fantastical story that has no basis in reality. This can destroy a relationship.

Love Avoidance and Love Addiction

Desperation for a lifetime commitment, and its opposite, total avoidance of a lifetime commitment, have been termed *love addiction* and *love avoidance*. Both dysfunctional psychological extremes are rooted in childhood issues and must be uprooted with the help of a professional who has been specifically trained in this area. Pia Mellody's book *Facing Love Addiction* and Terrence Real's book *I Don't Want to Talk About It* deal specifically with these issues. If you want either to "cling to" or "run from" a good relationship, these books are a must read!

One of the issues that causes love addiction is a child whose parent or parents were not available to adequately nurture the child. This can be physical unavailability, such as the death of a parent, or a parent being gone a majority of the time either because of work demands or overinvolvement in social interest. Love addiction can also occur if a parent is physically available but not emotionally connected with a child. An example of this is a father who sits in his La-Z-Boy chair drinking Bud Light and demanding that his television watching not be interrupted by the children wanting to talk or needing help with a task. Anything that keeps a parent or parents physically, emotionally, or psychologically away from the family can be a scary for a child. When this occurs, the absence can create a fear of abandonment and/or or fear of being alone.

Even as the child grows into adulthood, the cognitive and emotional memories can be lodged in the adult's body. The panic feeling of fear of abandonment can resurface when the adult faces a painful breakup or a relationship that fizzles out. I have had many adults come to see me saying that a breakup caused panic attacks and constant anxiety. When they tell me that they feel abandoned, I remind them that they cannot be abandoned. If we left them on the front porch, they could get up and walk away. An adult can be left, but *not* abandoned. The technique that I use to heal this childhood wound is to reconnect the adult with the wounded child, thus disempowering the child-hood fear.

Love avoidance and the fear of commitment is created when a parent uses a child to caretake a parent's emotional needs and well-being. This is called emotional incest. Even though I discussed emotional incest in chapter 2, it is worth repeating because of the way it creates love avoidance and the fear of commitment. When emotional incest occurs, the child is given the message that it is their job is to make a parent feel proud, happy, safe, etc. A parent's job is always to take care of the child's emotional needs by nurturing the child with love, validation, and support so that they can focus on age-appropriate activities and relationships.

Emotional incest causes a child to be enmeshed with his parent. This means that there is no separateness. The parent believes that he is a reflection of the child's feelings and behaviors and the child is a reflection of the parent's feelings and behaviors. It is not uncommon for an adult to assume that if his parent committed a crime or committed suicide that he is doomed to a similar behavior. Emotional incest is very detrimental to a child because if a child is parenting his parent, then he is being robbed of his own emotional childhood. Not only is the child prevented from being a child emotionally, the parent is not available to focus on parenting the child.

Examples of emotional incest that you or another child may experience:

—You misbehaved and your parent made a statement such as, "I feel so disappointed in you. I cannot believe that you would do this to me."

An appropriate parenting statement would be, "It is not OK to hit your sister and I feel angry. It is my anger and I will deal with it. I do want that behavior to stop."

—Your father said to you, "I am going out of town and you need to take care of your mother and keep her happy."

An appropriate parenting statement would be, "I am going out of town. Your mom will be here to take care of you. I hope you have a good couple of days."

—Your parents got their feelings hurt because you wanted to spend time with your friends rather than with them.

In this case, you were expected to keep your parents from feeling sad or lonely.

—Your parents expected you to behave in a way that was beyond your capability because of age or cognitive development.

—Your parents needed you to behave in a certain way so that they could feel happy rather than angry or embarrassed. Examples of this are: taking you, as a three-year-old, out to a prolonged dinner and expecting you to sit still and be quiet; expecting you as a two-year-old not to touch items on a coffee table; expecting you and your siblings not to have disagreements; expecting you to be responsible for your siblings.

—Your parents said, "I am so disappointed in you."

This is an extremely shaming message; it rips the child to the core of his essence. It tells the child that he has failed to fulfill his duty to make his parent feel happy or proud. It is not the child's job to make his parent feel anything.

Emotional incest is particularly shame producing because the task set before the child is impossible. Adults are responsible for their own emotional reality. When a child is unable to satisfy a parent's needs the child will feel extremely sad or guilty because he has failed at creating happiness, pride, or love in his parents, the people he loves the most. That is a monumental job and can produce a lot of fear within the child because he is emotionally and physically dependent on his parents for survival. It is like water-skiing behind a boat that no one is driving! If he cannot please his parents, the child fears possible withdrawal of the attention and love he so desperately needs, thus creating a fear of abandonment that will be carried into adulthood.

Emotional incest also causes a child to feel inadequate and like a failure. It creates the need to be an emotional care-taker, a people pleaser, and a dutiful son/daughter. The child will believe that it is his job to "fix" anyone who is feeling sadness, fear, anger, guilt, or shame. He will absorb the un-comfortable feelings of family and friends, perceive these feelings as being his own, and then make behavioral choices based on the absorbed feelings.

The way this often plays out in adult relationships is that the person who grew up feeling responsible for his parents emotionally will have trouble maintaining a relationship. After about the three-month mark of a new relationship, when there might be a discussion or disagreement about an issue, the person who grew up in a family that was en-meshed will get triggered, and the historical, dutiful feeling of emotionally caretaking can be overwhelming. When this happens, the triggered person will often end the relation-ship in order to escape the feelings of having to caretake another person.

I always tell people that rather than run away from the re-lationship, all they have to do is realize that they are not responsible for emotionally caretaking anyone. I use the same technique that I use with love addiction by rescuing the wounded child and telling that child that it is *never* the child's job to emotionally take care of another adult This is how a love avoidant learns how to breathe and stay in a good relationship.

If both parties have worked on any fear of abandonment or love-avoidant issues and they have looked at some of their family of origin issues, then they are both probably starting to feel pretty confident that this could be their forever person. When this occurs, there is a level of satisfaction, relief, and excitement that overtakes the relationship. The couple will take great joy in daydreaming and discussing the wonderful possibilities that lie ahead.

Discuss Wedding and Honeymoon Details

The importance of discussing the logistics of a wedding and a honeymoon cannot be overemphasized. Whether this is your first, second, or third wedding, you both need to agree upon who is paying for what, where, and when. Just because there are many traditions around the division of wedding duties and payments, it does not mean that these traditions have to be followed. For example, the bride's family usually pays for the wedding dress, wedding invitations, flowers, reception, and sometimes the bridesmaids' dresses while the groom or the grooms family pays for the rehearsal dinner and honeymoon. These expenses can become overwhelming to the bride, groom, and their families, so as unglamorous and potentially contentious as this may seem, each party must be transparent and honest about what they are willing to contribute to the big or small event. Saying yes when you want to say no will often lead to resentment, and a marriage with a foundation of resentment will probably crumble. If it does last, it will not be a picnic filled with joy and laughter.

The Gritty

Prenuptial Agreement

An often particularly sticky subject in premarital negotiations is the possible need or desire for a prenuptial agreement. Most who require a prenup do so because of assets. If you go down the prenup path, it's essential that each person totally understands what the document says. At this stage in the relationship, a divorce may seem impossible to comprehend. But if fifteen years down the road, Mr. You-Thought-He-Was-Forever decides to exit the marriage for a skanky younger woman, then you do not want to shift from living life free of financial worries into a life as Little Orphan Annie.

The basic elements of most prenuptial agreements include:

1. Protections against the debts of the other spouse
2. Distinction between marital and separate property
3. Provisions for children from previous marriages
4. Protections from estate plans along with creating wills, living trusts, and other estate documents for your family's future
5. Descriptions of each spouse's monetary responsibilities
6. A possible "sunset clause," which voids the agreement after a specified period of time

Awe, the Bliss and Blain of Blending Families

If this is your second rodeo and one of you or both of you have children, there are many issues that need discussed. Who pays for what? Who corrects the child when he or she is not your child? Who makes the rules for bedtime, acceptable television shows, household chores, home-work, and iPad usage? Can you have different rules for different families? These are real-life potential sources of conflict in a marriage, so dealing with some of them before you walk down the aisle can prevent a lot of early marriage discord.

Here are a few thoughts that can help a couple ease into the "one big happy family" idea as they blend all of the different personalities, ages, and different genders.

- Make sure that you are nurturing your marriage re-lationship along with being effective parents. Make honest communication and having fun with one an-other a daily priority. The marriage does not need to come before the children, but at the same time, put-ting your marriage on the back burner will turn the marriage passion into ashes!
- Be patient and keep open-minded perspective about one another's children. The blending process cannot be forced, and it will take time for everyone to get used to all of the different personalities.
- Utilize the experiences of your friends and family members that have traveled this path before you.

- Spend one-on-one time with each of the children. Ask questions about how they are doing and be sure to talk about feelings.
- Have a family discussion about what the children need or want to call the stepparent. This is how they will introduce the stepparent to others. Most adults will prefer that their partner's children call them by their first name. For example, my stepson called me Janice and would introduce me as his stepmother, Janice. Never force a stepchild into referring to their stepparent as Dad or Mom.
- Intertwine some of each families' traditions along with creating new holiday and special event traditions for the blended family.
- Develop a team mentality with polite common courtesies such as "Hello," "Goodbye," How are you?" "How is your day? " "Please," and "Thank you." Beyond this, do not force communication. Children at different ages have different comfort levels regarding chitchat. For example, an eight-year-old might be extremely comfortable with extended dialog, while a twelve-year-old might me unwilling to communicate with very little detail beyond one- or two-word responses. Both of these examples are age appropriate.
- Anticipate bumps in the road and when they appear; do not overreact. When at all possible, try to discipline and discuss poor behavior in private. This will prevent the child who is in trouble from feeling embarrassed and shamed. And *no* yelling and spanking!

- Make your scheduled visitation with you children your #1 priority.
- As you embark on this new family adventure, stay connected with old friendships and social connections. Practice the idea of the lyrics to the song I learned in Brownies and Girl Scouts: "Make new friends and keep the old. One is silver and the other gold."

Parenting Styles

Parenting style is an area worth discussing as two people contemplate blending families. The goal of effective parenting is to help the child remain safe and to support healthy growth and development. The way in which you parent can affect everything from how much your child weighs to how he or she feels about themself. It's important to practice effective parenting skills because the way you interact with your child and how you discipline him or her will influence them for the rest of their life.

Through extensive research, experts have identified four basic types of parenting styles:

- Authoritarian
- Authoritative
- Permissive
- Uninvolved

Not only is it important to understand which style of parenting each of you have practiced with you own children but also which style you will practice as you blend your families or have additional children together.

Authoritarian parenting lives by the sayings, "My way or the highway" and "Because I said so." This type of parenting does not allow any room for the child to develop and state their opinions or reasons why they disagree with the stance that the parent has taken. The household operates under the "a rule is a rule" mentality and does not give the child an opportunity to have a voice if that voice disagrees. When a child is raised in this type of environment, there is a high possibility that the child may become hostile, aggressive, and defiant. The child may also start to lie and disobey the household rules as a way to act out against the parents' unwillingness to even hear the child's position. Under these circumstances, the parents are teaching the child that their thoughts are wrong even before that child has had an opportunity to speak their thoughts. Authoritarian parenting will typically focus on punishment rather than teaching the child how to develop self-discipline and self-containment.

Authoritative parenting includes explanations as to why the household has a rule or why the parent is unwilling to allow the child to do something. If the child reacts negatively to hearing no, the parent understands that most people do not like to be told no, and the parent does not expect the child to respond with something like, "Gee, Dad, thank you for telling me no. You must love me a lot and want me to be safe."

Children are not supposed to be grateful for hearing no. Even if the child gets mad or cries, the parent can just simply say, "I can tell that you are unhappy because I said that you could not ride your bike at night. I understand that you disagree with my decision, but I simply love you too much to risk you getting injured." Part of becoming an effective parent is learning to be OK when other people are not OK.

In this environment, the focus is on maintaining a communicative and positive relationship and listening to the child's reasoning no matter how ridiculous it might seem to the parent. Being in this type of environment provides an opportunity for teaching the child to be comfortable even in the midst of opposing opinions. In an authoritative parenting environment, positive reinforcement is the mainstay of communication and learning. This will help the children to become responsible adults.

Permissive parenting style has very few rules and expectations of children. Even though the parents are loving and express caring about their children, they don't see their children as mature or capable enough to carry out certain tasks or responsibilities that require self-control.

Along with avoiding confrontation whenever possible, permissive parents rarely discipline their children. Instead of trying to prevent problems from happening by setting rules and expectations they allow their children to figure things out for themselves.

Uninvolved parenting includes parents who tend to act emotionally distant from their children. Because the parents are overwhelmed by their own problems, they limit interactions with their children. As a result, the parents will provide little or no supervision, and set no expectations or demands for particular behaviors.

These parents will show very little love and affection and will frequently skip school and extra- curricular events, along with parent-teacher conferences.

- Act emotionally distant from their children
- Limit interactions with their children because they're too overwhelmed by their own problems
- Provide little or no supervision
- Set few or no expectations or demands for behavior
- Show little warmth, love, and affection towards their children
- Skip school events and parent-teacher conferences

Kevin

"My boyfriend told me to go out and get something that makes him look sexy, so I came back drunk."
—Anonymous

It had been two years since I had last seen Kevin, and I was really looking forward to his visit. When he first came to see me, he was a bit of a mess. He had just broken up with a guy who cheated on him several times, and he was really struggling with his shame about his sexuality. To make matters even more difficult, Kevin's father could not wrap his brain around the fact that his only son was gay. Along with the family rejection, the fundamentalist church that his family attended had disowned him. Kevin realized that he was spiraling downward into depression, so he continued to see me weekly as he worked diligently at healing his deep childhood shame core.

After three months, he was ready to get back into the dating world and see where life would take him.

When Kevin walked into my office, he was accompanied by a very handsome man who immediately grinned from ear to ear and said, "My name is Michael. So I finally get to meet the amazing woman who is responsible for helping to heal Kevin, my husband and the love of my life."

"Oh, my goodness," I responded. "I am thrilled to meet you! When Kevin made this appointment, he told me that he had a surprise for me, and I guess your and Kevin's marriage is the surprise. I am absolutely thrilled for both of you!"

After a few minutes of talking about how Kevin and Michael met, I asked, "So how do your individual families feel about you guys getting married?"

Kevin quickly answered, "Well, you will not believe it, but my mother, sisters, and yes, even my father are very happy to have Michael in our family. They all love him."

"That is so fabulous, Kevin! What happened to change your father's position about you being gay?"

"My father had a so-called near death experience while having a massive heart attack shortly after Michael and I met. He says that he saw God and that God told him how much God loves him and loves me. God

also told him that he was not ready for heaven so he needed to right the wrongs of his past and treat everyone with love. He was on a ventilator for two weeks, and then shortly after he got out of the hospital, he asked me to come over so that we could have a chat about something. I was hesitant to sit down with my father to chat because I was afraid that we would have another one of those 'you are going to hell, Kevin, if you do not de-gay yourself' knock-down drag-out screaming matches."

"So did you go?" I asked.

*"Yes, I did," Kevin proudly proclaimed. "Because of the work you I had done around rescuing the little boy, me, along with healing all of that 'gay' shame that had plagued me for twenty years, I was no longer afraid of my father. I realized that I could leave the conversation and walk out of my parents' house at any time if my father chose to belittle or berate me in any way. I remembered you telling me that as an adult, I could not get in trouble, I could not get a spanking, and I could not get grounded. I cannot even begin to tell you how much that freed me from the fear that had previously paralyzed me from standing up and walking away from my father's rage. I also remembered your acronym for fear: **F**-false or future, **E**-experiences, **A**-appearing, **R**-real."*

"So what did your father say to you when you went to his house?" I asked.

"Well, for the first five minutes, he cried like baby. After he pulled himself together, he began to talk about the way his father had treated him. My grandfather was actually the sheriff in his small hometown, and he was known as being a racist and merciless when it came to treating people who had violated a law. My father also told me that his father had been emotionally and verbally abusive to my grandmother and my aunt, and physically abusive to my father by pushing him, slapping him in the face, and spanking him with a belt.

"My father said that because he was not as violent as his father, then he must have been doing OK. My father also told me that my mother told him that if he did not accept the fact that I was gay and continued to berate and shame me, that she was going to file for divorce. I could not believe that my mother had that kind of courage to draw a line in the sand with my father. At any rate, that must have done the trick, because my father has become a different person. Every day he calls and tells Michael and me how much he loves us. He actually told me that he would pay for us to go on a honeymoon and that he hopes that Michael and I will adopt a child or obtain a surrogate so that we could have a child and he could have a grandchild. We

found a surrogate, and Michael and I are expecting a baby girl in four months. How crazy is all of that?"

"Well, actually that is pretty crazy and also fabulous!" I responded. "Miracles happen every day, and that is what has happened in your family's life. Kevin, you've done a lot of heavy psychological lifting in healing that little boy's shame, and now you are experiencing the results of your work. You, Michael, and your families have a lot of joyful experiences ahead, and I want you both to know that you deserve all of the goodness that your precious hearts can handle. I cannot wait to meet your daughter!"

"We are both so excited," said Kevin. "I have never been this happy in my entire life. Michael and I really want to make sure that we treat one another with respect and kindness."

Michael nodded his head in agreement and then asked, "Would you be willing to meet with Kevin and I once or twice a month so that we can keep this good relationship going strong?"

"Absolutely, Michael," I said. "I would be honored to help you guys to keep the fire alive in your marriage. I always tell couples that a good relationship is not like fairy dust falling from heaven. Rather, it is the implementation

of a set of skills. You guys maintaining a great relationship will be the greatest gift that you could possibly give to that precious daughter of yours. I will see you next month!"

Chapter 9
Keeping the Fire Alive

Pay Attention to Your Intention

After tying the knot, it's extremely important to maintain the integrity of the relationship with the goal to having good and stable marriage. A good marriage is not something that happens to you like fairy dust falling from the heavens. It's something that you create with intention and attention. I strongly suggest that couples write down descriptions that encapsulate their definition of a good marriage and make those their intention. For example: "Our good marriage will include kindness, safety, fun, honesty, and flexibility." As each person discusses how that would look behaviorally, the intention of the marriage will take form. The goal will then be for both individuals to pay attention and take responsibility for their own behavior relative to the agreed-upon intention.

Even with the best of intentions, there will be occasional conflicts in the marriage. In his best-selling book, *The New*

Rules of Marriage, Terrence Real does a fantastic job of discussing the process of repair and the tools for making a marriage work. I have had the privilege of training under Terry for many years, and I use his techniques when working with couples and in my own marriage as well.

Family of Origin

Another issue that frequently arises is conflict with one another's family of origin. When individuals get married, there can be an internal conflict regarding a primary loyalty issue with their new spouse and the family of origin, particularly a parent. For example, a mother wants her son to FaceTime her every day when he and his wife are on vacation, and this duty takes precedence over the plans that the wife wants to make for other activities. It is vitally important that the mother is *not* the man's primary concern. She can be a concern, just not his *primary* concern. As difficult as it may be to disappoint the mother, the wife must feel she's the number one woman in his life. Enmeshment with a parent is not attractive at all, and it will have a hugely negative effect on the marriage... especially in your sex life.

The Pyramid of Primary Loyalty

Below you can see an image of the "pyramid of primary loyalty" that can provides the reader with a better understating of this concept.

In the very top section of the pyramid are the couple and any underage children.

On the next lower section are adult children and other family members, including grandchildren, grandparents, and parents.

Then the broad bottom section includes all other individuals in the couple's life. Of course, different levels can be added, and the people can be moved around, except for the top level, which must remain restricted.

When I show my clients this layout, some people have a difficult time thinking about an unhappy parent, realizing that they are not at the top with their spouse. I gently remind them that making their spouse feel that they, along with any underage children, are the most important people in their life will go a long way to creating a happy, successful marriage.

Triangle of Primary Loyalty

COUPLE

UNDERAGE CHILDREN

ADULT CHILDREN, PARENTS,

GRANDPARENTS, GRANDCHILDREN

ANY OTHER INDIVIDUALS IN THE COUPLE'S LIFE

175

Fan the Sexual Fire

An important aspect of a lifetime of happiness is to remember that your sex life needs to be vital and fun. I strongly recommend that couples have quarterly getaways in order to spice up their sex life. There is something magical about having a romantic dinner at a nice restaurant and then going to a hotel room for the night. I always suggest that the woman buy new lingerie, make a hotel reservation, check in early, put rose petals on the bed, and send her Mr. Marvelous a text or email with the address of the hotel, room number, and an alluring note. Changing your zip code will put some extra zip your lovemaking.

By the way, don't forget about long, lingering foreplay!

In chapter 6, I discussed the four types of intimacy: emotional intimacy, intellectual intimacy, physical intimacy, sexual intimacy. Not only are all of these areas of intimacy essential to keeping the sexual fire alive in a committed relationship, but they also build upon one another, which creates a wall of emotional, intellectual, physical, and sexual safety. Here is an example of how building a wall of safety looks in a relationship.

Sally and John dated for three years before they decided to get married. During their dating they found out a lot about one another. Although they had many things in common, they also had several differences. Because Sally had grown up in a household that was politically very conservative, she typically voted for the Republican Party candidates. John, on the other hand, grew up in a more liberal environment, which predisposed him to vote for the Democratic Party candidates. Even though they sometimes had fairly intense conversations about some issues, they quickly realized that they could agree to disagree without damaging the integrity of the relationship.

When Sally and John did disagree on issues, they were each able to express and listen to one another's opinions and thoughts (intellectual intimacy). They were also both able to name and control their own feelings (emotional intimacy), thus avoiding demeaning statements to one another out of anger or fear. If a discussion started to escalate, they had a previously agreed upon "signal," which either person could use as a way to say, "I need to leave this conversation because it is getting too intense." They also had a previous agreement that when one or the other used "the signal," a handshake, hug, and or kiss ended the discussion (physical intimacy).

This is an example of how couples can use intellectual intimacy, emotional intimacy, and physical intimacy as building blocks to create safety in a relationship. The occurrence of this sort of interaction improves sexual intimacy because each person feels that they are safe to be themself. Being treated with respect and the understanding that "you are not wrong because you are different from me" is easy to reciprocate, thus creating a boomerang effect, which fuels love and sexual intimacy. When a woman feels emotionally,

177

intellectually, and physically safe with a man, it makes it easier for her to be vulnerable enough to take her clothes off. This safety also helps to empower her to feel spontaneous, adventuresome, and confident between the sheets!

And it's worth repeating...don't forget about foreplay!

Nurturing the Other Three Domains of Intimacy

Emotional Intimacy

Everyone likes to hear compliments from their partner. Unfortunately, a lot of people are more comfortable complaining about what they are not getting rather than verbalizing some of the positive attributes that their partner brings to the table. Telling one another how much you appreciate and admire specific traits and behaviors will always help to bring a couple closer.

The majority of people find it easy to say "thank you" for gifts and extravagant efforts and yet, sometimes saying, "thank you" for the smaller efforts will have an even greater impact. For example, telling your partner how much you appreciate that they help to clean up the kitchen after dinner or telling your partner how much you appreciate how hard they work to provide for the family will always have a positive effect on a relationship.

Another element of building emotional intimacy is practicing forgiveness. People who harbor resentments create insurmountable negative energy in their relationships. Not only will the negative energy make it impossible to have a fun and happy relationship, but it can also make people physically ill. Forgiveness is a gift that we give ourselves.

Things to practice:

- Make it a daily habit to tell your partner at least one specific thing you admire or appreciate about them. If you have children, do the same thing with them. They will love it!
- When you notice that your partner looks pretty or handsome, make sure and compliment them on their appearance.
- Forgive easily.

Physical Intimacy

Physical intimacy can be described as being physically connected without having the purpose of promoting sex. Even though physical touch can sometimes lead to sexual touch, a healthy couple will be able to connect physically without an underlying sexual motive. Women will sometimes avoid physical touch because they are afraid that their partner will take the physical touch as a sexual advance. It is very important for both people to understand that they have the ability and the right say no to sexual touch if that is not what they want.

Things to practice:

- Hold hands
- Hug
- Give and receive massage
- Sit close together on the couch
- Kiss good night
- Kiss good morning
- Never stop dating
- Make a list of the things that you really like about your partner and then read it to them.
- Surprise your partner

Intellectual Intimacy

The two main components of intellectual intimacy are speaking and listening. In a healthy relationship, it is important that both partners learn how to speak skillfully and non-offensively to one another as well as learning how to be an active listener.

In order to preserve the integrity of a relationship, it is vitally important that we are mindful of the way we speak to one another. In simple matters like discussing the activities of the day or having a conversation about noncontroversial world events and issues, we do not necessarily need to be careful with our words. On the other hand, if I want to discuss something that is potentially volatile, I want to start the conversation by asking my partner if this time is good time to discuss something.

If my partner agrees that the time is good, then I will begin my statements with "I…"

For example, I might say, "I would like you to…", or "I feel…", or "I want…." These are examples of speaking non-offensively and noncritically. When we criticize someone for something, we have set the stage for defensiveness, blame, and shame, which always creates a divide in the relationship. The listener will typically shut down or become aggressive. Conflict resolution should *never* be about winning or losing, because if one person wins and another loses, then the relationship loses. Make sure that you are asking for what you want instead of criticizing what you are getting.

The second essential element of intellectual intimacy is learning how to be an "active listener." The term *active listening* is used to describe the practice of consciously hearing both the words and meaning of the message that the speaker is trying to convey. In order to really hear and understand the speaker, the listener must pay attention to the words, the underlying meaning and the body language of the speaker. The active listener should also let the speaker know that they are being heard by looking at the speaker and eliminating anything that is a distraction.

Things to practice:

When speaking,

- Be kind with your tone and words.

- Be gently honest.
- Ask for what you want.

When listening,

- Look at the speaker.
- Don't form your defense while listening.
- Eliminate distracting factors such as phones and television.
- Nod to demonstrate that the speaker is being heard.
- Use facial expressions to convey that you are listening.
- Interject words such as "yes, un huh, oh my," etc., which show you are following the speaker.
- Provide a summary for clarification if needed.

Other fun ideas that fuel connectedness through intellectual intimacy:

- Daydream and talk about your individual and mutual goals.
- Reminisce about how you met and your first date.
- Reminisce about your first kiss.
- Make individual bucket lists.
- Make a mutual bucket list.
- Text once or twice during the day.
- Do little, unexpected things for your partner.

Connecting with a Higher Being

Along with the four types of intimacy, I also believe that developing a shared spiritual connection with a Higher Power is paramount to experiencing a rich and abundant relationship. Considering the possibility that something larger than you exists (such as a loving Divine Intelligence who wants you to experience life to the fullest) is tremendously helpful in overcoming the belief that you do not deserve an abundant relationship.

For most people, the thought that you must do it all on your own is overwhelming. It is entirely too much pressure. You will feel a great sense of relief and security in knowing that there is a loving power that runs through the universe and is willing and able to provide you with guidance, opportunity, and endless acceptance. It matters not what name you give to your Higher Power. Call it God, the Universe, Energy, a Life Force, Nature, or whatever your intuition tells you is right for you. Some people find it easier to connect with a Higher Power that is a "she" rather than a "he." It is what it is, regardless of shape, size, name, or gender.

Serendipity is, in my opinion, your ability to tap into the opportunities that have been placed in your path by your Higher Power. They are not there by accident. They are there to help provide you with the ways and means of achieving your goals and receiving the desires of your heart.

You and your partner may find it easy to believe in the existence of Divine Intelligence. If so, then you were likely raised by parents who had mainstream spiritual beliefs, or perhaps you attended a church that spoke of an unconditionally loving God who does not judge. If you are one of those people, cheers! The process of understanding that you deserve and will be led to experience abundance is much easier for you. If this is not the case for you, the process may be slightly more difficult. But take heart—with a little time and effort, you will be able to grow into your own spiritual knowing.

If you or your partner were raised in a religious system that was shame based, you may need to reconstruct a new concept of God. This was my experience. Although the word "God" felt right for me, I knew that I needed to completely let go of a judgmental God and create a loving God.

I accomplished this in a couple of ways.

First, I decided that I needed to start from scratch. I determined that the shame-based messages I had heard were totally false and were fear based. Because I had been an avid Bible student, I went through the Bible and wrote down on index cards only the scriptures that had to do with God's love. I carried those cards in my purse so that I could read them whenever the opportunity arose. There is no telling how many times I read those cards. I literally had to brainwash myself into a different conviction that consisted solely of a loving God.

Second, I decided to read books about other religions and different concepts of spirituality. I read about Buddhism and other Eastern philosophies. I read the Bhagavad Gita, the Koran, and books by Wayne W. Dyer, Marianne Williamson, Deepak Chopra, and Thomas Merton, to name only a few. What I came to believe was that everyone was basically saying the same thing; they just worded it differently.

I also became an observer of nature, recognizing that the beauty of nature and the miracles apparent in the very existence of that beauty represented God's love. I came to believe that God was God and that this Power loved me and thought that I rocked! It was that simple. I loved my new awareness as it settled into my soul. I continue to keep it really simple because my mind can get carried away with trying to figure it all out. When my mind tries to be too "smart," I can start to doubt, and I don't want that to happen. I shifted from a belief into a knowing that I felt permeating every cell in my body. I still have that feeling. It literally runs through my veins and is my life force. Searching for your own truth will be worth the effort, so start searching.

Once you and your partner come to settle into a belief that feels comfortable, you have begun to experience a spiritual awakening. You are learning to understand that you are spiritual beings having human experiences. You may both start to believe that you are extensions of your Higher Power, and you can recognize that others are an extension of their Higher Power.

We are all connected because we are all "of" the same source. We are literally brothers and sisters with every other human being. As you connect with an all-loving Divine Being, you will begin to have faith in the goodness of life, no matter how it all appears. Faith will give you hope—hope for today and hope for tomorrow. I love the following definition of faith:

> To trust in the force that moves the universe is faith.
> Faith isn't blind; it's visionary.
> Faith is believing that the universe is on our side and that the universe knows what it's doing.
> Faith is a psychological awareness of an unfolding force for good, constantly at work in all dimensions.
> —Author unknown

Your spiritual journey will last a lifetime as it continues to change and grow. I suggest that you start and end your day with spiritual readings so that you stay tuned into your spiritual awareness. Once you taste it, you cannot be separated from it. Even if you occasionally do not feel it, it is there. Stay in your practice of spirituality and you will feel it again.

Kristie

"I want to get you excited about who you are, what you are, what you have, and what can still be for you. I want to inspire you to see that you can go far beyond where you are right now."
—Virginia Satir

I grew up in a very chaotic household. My father was an alcoholic who was never available emotionally and was obsessed with saving money. He always said we were poor, even though he made millions of dollars. This was very confusing to me as a child. My mother was an emotional mess who was obsessed with trying to stop my father from drinking. Pretty much, we did not have parents or caregivers. Luckily, I had two sisters, one older and one younger, who were there to support me. We were all very close and are still close to this day. My parents ended up getting a divorce when I was fifteen years old, but most of the shame and abuse had already occurred.

I was a wounded child. I was always very

scared and could never sleep alone at night. I thought that someone was going to kidnap me or murder me. Since my parents were not there to comfort me, I had to survive on my own. The only thing that made my anxiety go away and made me feel safe was to make all of my "stuff" perfect. I developed obsessive-compulsive disorder (OCD), and when my life felt out of control, my OCD and perfectionism would get out of control. I never realized that this behavior was not coming from the "adult" me but from the wounded child within me. It saved my life to heal the inner child and to comfort her. Now she knows that the adult me is here to always take care of her. She has nothing to fear.

After working to heal the shame, I began to use affirmations to help shape me into a healthy adult. They truly became the source for restructuring my thinking. I put the affirmations in a place where I could see them and read them daily so they could become a part of me and my everyday life. Whenever I would start to doubt myself or feel shame creeping back into my soul, I'd say the affirmations over and over so they could become embedded in my brain. Previously I had read sayings once or twice and thought they would become part of my everyday living. However, once I healed the shame, everything changed and made sense. I realized my self-value and could, therefore, truly understand and believe the affirmations.

The affirmations are my saving grace and the template of how I want to live my new, healthy life. I am now operating as an adult and not like a child. I realize that the affirmations can become a part of my life, not just something I read. I understand that I had to totally believe that my Higher Power was my partner and would always be with me. I am not perfect, and I know that there will be hard days. That is part of the human experience. But now I know I am never alone. At all times I have my "child self" dancing on my shoulder with God next to me leading us through life.

—Kristie

Chapter 10
Realizing Your Heart's Desire

Yes, This Is Really Possible

Enough time has been spent on the heavy lifting. You have examined your baggage, taken what you want to keep, and left the rest. It is time to put your baggage in storage and move on to the lighter part of life that is waiting for you with open arms.

You want to be happy, right? If the answer is yes, then it is important for you to decide what it is that will bring you happiness. These are the things that you want to attract into your life. The Universe has no limitations, so do not hold yourself back. The Universe is also plentiful, so do not concern yourself with whether or not there is enough to go around for everyone. It is never wrong to want something more or something different from what you currently have, so dream big.

The mind is a powerful tool, so picturing what you want has an amazing power to create. Remember that Divine Intelligence has your best interests at heart. If you don't get exactly what you want, you will get something better. "Not my will but Thy will" is a strong way to let go and allow your Higher Power to do its job.

The importance of taking action cannot be overstated. The actions you take in the general direction of what you desire will create the emotional energy that will help to jump-start the abundance process. There are several steps that will help you get the process started. As you implement the following suggestions, either individually or with your partner, you will begin to see yourself and your relationship in a new way, a way of abundance, prosperity, and fullness.

Step 1: Write Down Desires, Wants, and Goals

The first step in attracting what you desire is to write down what you want to experience and have in your life. The written word is very powerful and provides a road map to follow. Be specific in your desires because a specificity will create excitement as you visualize your future. It will put a zip in your step as you anticipate the good.

Write about the areas in your life where you would like to experience improvements; these could include finances, career, health, relationships, personal or spiritual growth, or material desires. Use descriptive words and be as thorough as you can. You may want something as simple as a new

191

dress. Write down what color you imagine the dress to be, the fabric it is made of, its particular style, and any special detailing it might have.

You may desire something bigger like your prefect mate, a new career, or a new house for yourself or your family. Make a list of the characteristics you desire and find appealing. If you desire a new house for your family you might write, "The house is a red brick colonial with white columns on a huge front porch. There are at least four bedrooms and three bathrooms, with plenty of room to entertain friends and loved ones. It has a large yard where my children can play, and it's furnished to my taste and satisfaction. The neighborhood is safe and quiet. The money to pay for it comes easily."

You can go to the river of abundance with
either a thimble or a barrel. The choice is yours.

Although all things are possible, some things are more prob-able than others. I love to sing and dance, and I would love to perform in a Broadway musical. At age seventy, however, it is not very probable. What I could do is be open to local theater if that were truly one of my heart's desires. Divine Intelligence can make a way where we can see no way, so dream big and be open to the unknown. Don't get tied up in the details of how it will come to pass. It is not up to the hu-man spirit to assume the order of how things happen. Have faith that your request has been heard and will be met in the right time and the right way. This is crucial. Get excited about going to the river of abundance with a barrel and know that your heart's desires are coming to you now in the best way possible.

Step 2: Make a "Vision Board"

A vision board is a success map of your heart's desires. It is a visual representation of your specific goals, wants, and desires. It takes the mental pictures of what you desire and makes them visible. After you have written your desires, find photos or pictures that portray them. Use pictures that are colorful and descriptive. The Universe thrives on color. Just look around you—there is color everywhere. If you want a big, colorful life, use pictures that depict that life.

Create a board that can be divided into the areas of your life in which you desire change, such as finances/career, love/relationships, personal/spiritual growth, health. For example, if you long for financial growth, add play money or checks to the board. No amount is too big. Perhaps you desire a dream home. Find photos that look similar to your dream home. If you cannot find an accurate representation, add pictures that might show specific details or elements of your new home. If you desire a new mate, look for a picture of a person you find attractive who might meet your specific criteria. Although you may not find the exact house or marry the person in your picture, the Universe uses the pictures as a reference point so that it can go to work on meeting your specific requirements. Again, vibrant color pictures will more quickly set your dreams into action.

When making a vision board, be creative and leave plenty of space for additional desires. Make more than one vision board if needed. It is perfectly acceptable to create multiple success maps. Perhaps you have one for your family, one for your career, and one for material desires. After you have completed your vision board, place it somewhere you can reflect on it frequently, such as your bathroom mirror or a special place where you feel spiritually connected. Ponder your rich and rewarding life as it unfolds before your eyes.

As the Universe begins to fulfill your wishes, mark them off your wish list or write "Done" on that vision board item. Remember to thank your Higher Power for bringing you your heart's desires. Gratitude for what you have will bring you more of what you want. You will be amazed to see how quickly you start to see changes as life unfolds to bring you your longings.

Step 3: Visualize It: See It to Be It

Now that you have mapped out your desired path on your vision board, it is important to set aside five to ten minutes each day to focus clearly on your new destiny. By visualizing what you wish to receive, you will further solidify your coming abundance. It is best to visualize in a quiet, private space. I visualize in the morning (after I have had my cup of coffee, of course), but if you are usually rushed in the morning, later in the day may be better for you. I also set a timer so that I am not tempted to look at the clock. Sit in a comfortable chair and shut your eyes. Think about living the abundant life that you have laid out in words and pictures. Make sure that you see yourself in the picture. What are you wearing? How is your hair styled? Feel the feelings that you will experience once you are living your dream. Do you have a gigantic smile on your face? Are tears of joy streaming down your face? The feelings are very important because they will turbo-charge change.

Visualize your desires accurately and vividly. For example, if you want a beautiful new car, picture yourself walking up to it. Open the door and get inside. What does the car smell like? Take in the features. Picture yourself driving to a particular destination. Maybe you are driving through the mountains or to the beach. What are you feeling? How does the car respond to your input? Are you listening to your favorite rock band or are you driving in silence? Is your family in the car or are you driving alone? Visualize any thoughts or feelings that will better connect you to your beautiful new car.

While visualizing your new life, you might think of something new or different that you want. Write it down and add it to your vision board so the Universe can get to work on that also.

Step 4: Prepare to Receive Your Heart's Desires by Taking Action

Preparing to receive what you want to have in your world actually signals to yourself and the Universe that you believe your desires are coming to you. You are taking action in the general direction of your dreams. It is like preparing for an invited guest to arrive. For example, if you want a new car, clean out your garage. You would not park the car of your dreams in a dirty garage that is cluttered and messy. Visit car dealerships that sell the car you desire. Walk around the car lot and pick out the color you want. Sit in the car that you would choose if you were buying the car. Smell the leather and feel the softness against your body. Take the car for a test drive and notice how you feel as you drive the car. Notice how the car handles the road. Be aware of how the steering wheel feels as you make a turn.

If you want to move into a different house, put your house on the market or drive around the neighborhood where you want to live. Notice the style of houses that you like. Can you see yourself living there? Clean out the drawers and cabinets in your current home, getting rid of the items that you would not take with you when you move.

If you want a new wardrobe, clean out your closet and donate the clothes that no longer suit you. You are helping others as well as making room for your new wardrobe. Walk around the store where you would buy your new wardrobe and notice the clothes that you would purchase. Feel the fabrics and even try on a few items so that you have a mental picture of yourself in the clothing.

If you desire a loving relationship, join a dating service or another group or activity where you will be around other single people with similar interests. Make a list of the characteristics that you want in your future partner. Notice the qualities in others that are important to you and work on having these same qualities yourself. Like attracts like. Visualize sitting on the couch or cooking dinner together in the kitchen. Think about how it will feel as you laugh and then embrace one another. Think about where you would travel together and collect pamphlets and pictures of that special place.

You would not order a hamburger and simply tell the cook to make it however he likes. You might not like it. Likewise, you would not order a partner (or any of your heart's desires) and leave the details up to fate.

If you take an action and it doesn't work, do not consider the action a failure. Think of the action as a stepping-stone toward abundance. What you experience today is not your tomorrow. Do not concern yourself with specific outcomes. Trust in the ultimate goodness of the Universe and believe that you deserve it. What you believe, you will receive!

Step 5: Abolish Doubt

As we've already discussed, negativity will block you from receiving what you want in your life. It is very important to eliminate as much negativity from your life as possible. Because the newspaper and news reports tend to dwell on negative things that are happening in our world, I strongly urge you to stop reading the newspaper and watching the news on television. It is especially important to not listen to negative news before you go to bed. If you fill your mind with the negativity of the day's tragic stories, it will be virtually impossible to follow with positive visualizations of what you want to come into your life. You will be taking one step forward and two steps back. You are sending yourself contradictory information when you listen to tragic stories and then try to focus on the good that is coming to you. Can you see how difficult it is to believe in your forthcoming financial abundance when you hear that the stock market fell one hundred points? If you do read the newspaper, just scan the headlines without reading all of the gory details. I have not read the newspaper, other than the sports section, in close to twenty years, and I have not missed it at all. What you really need to know will come to you.

It is equally important to stay away from negative people. There are many people who love to talk about their own misery and the misery of others. They frequently discuss disease, aging, and the failing relationships of their friends and families. When you find yourself in the midst of people who thrive on negativity, it would be in your best interest to excuse yourself or limit the amount of time you spend in their company. If you cannot get away from a discussion that turns negative, simply say to yourself, "That is not my reality" or "That may be your reality, but it is not mine." Limiting your exposure to negativity is a gift you can give yourself, and it will only accelerate your ability to receive divine abundance.

Step 6: Affirm It

Stating that your heart's desires already exist is a pathway to your abundance. Make a commitment to affirm daily what you want to have in your life. As you do so, thank the Universe for meeting your needs in perfect timing. By believing that your needs are already met, you can begin to live a life that is free—free from burdens, frustration, and lack. Confirm your abundance and know that you are taken care of perfectly.

Here is an example of a powerful affirmation:

With an open mind and willing heart, I bless my own process and I have faith that my needs are being met.

This is a very private practice. It isn't that it is a secret, but these are your own individual thoughts and desires. When you discuss your innermost wants and desires with others, their feedback and input can diminish your commitment to change. You can talk your way out of your own good. Do not try to convince others of your new awareness. Everyone has his own path. With an open mind and willing heart, bless your own process and have faith that your needs are being met. Your thoughts, wants, and desires are between you and your Higher Power.

Chapter II
Mantras and Affirmations

"We can never go back again, that much is certain."
—Daphne du Maurier

The following is a sampling of mantras and affirmations that will help you practice techniques for living abundantly. Feel free to write your own affirmations or make any changes to the ones below to better fit your wants and desires. Remember to state them in a positive light rather than focusing on what you have that you don't want. When you make a statement regarding what you have but don't want, you are feeding energy into what you do not want and the condition may very well stay with you. The statement "I am" is a simple and effective way to tell the Universe that you believe you deserve abundance.

Remember to take what works for you and leave what doesn't. References to "Divinity," "God," and "the Universe" represent and encompass your personal Higher Power, whatever that may be.

Abundance

I am now living life abundantly.

I deserve to experience divine abundance because I am a child of God.

Abundance is my birthright. I claim it for myself under grace and in God's perfect timing.

The financial abundance that flows through the Universe is my heritage. It comes to me now.

I believe in the goodness of God. God provides through me in perfect ways.

The Universe is my infinite supply. I am showered with plenty of all that I want and need.

I am gracefully connected to the river of abundance. My supply comes to me in perfect ways and in perfect timing.

I am able to spend money without fear, as I understand that God is my unfailing source.

I release all negative thinking as I claim my inheritance of abundance.

Unlimited abundance comes to me under grace and in perfect ways.

I celebrate God's abundance as I claim it for myself and those whom I love.

Unlimited abundance now comes to me in unlimited ways.

As I enter the promised land with grace, limitation and lack now fall away.

God is my immediate supply. All of my needs are now met in a perfect way.

Infinite Spirit, open the way for my great abundance now. I am an irresistible magnet for all that belongs to me by divine right.

I give thanks that abundance is mine by divine right. It now pours in and piles up, under grace and in perfect ways.

I cast this burden of lack on Christ, and I go free to have plenty.

I now thank God, the giver of good, for the gifts I am given.

The unexpected happens. My seemingly impossible good now comes to pass.

From the divine love that flows through my being, I call forth my abundance and prosperity in all forms that will bring.

Divine healing now comes to pass in my body. This is my rightful inheritance.

As I release all resentments, my cells are restored to their natural state of wholeness. I give thanks for my radiant health.

As I release the need to be right, I am restored to wholeness. Serenity is my birthright.

Let me now express the divine idea in my mind, body, and affairs.

I now act with motives of faith and not fear.

Thou in me art:

eternal joy
eternal youth
eternal wealth
eternal health
eternal love
eternal life

Nothing is too good to be true;

Nothing is too wonderful to happen;

Nothing is too good to last.

Relationships

I am manifesting my healthy relationship.

I give thanks for the divine partner that is coming into my life in God's perfect timing.

I deserve to experience an abundant relationship because I am a child of God.

I was created to be in a joyful relationship. I claim it now as my rightful inheritance.

I love myself. I love others. As a loving being, others love me.

I will attract that which I am. Therefore, as I develop within myself the traits that I deserve and want in a relationship, I will attract that perfect partner.

I am created in the image of God. Because God is love, I am love.

I joyfully wait for the arrival of my divinely chosen partner.

Divine love is maintained in my marriage, through me and for me.

Because I now know my preciousness, I am ready to love and to be loved.

All of my relationships are peaceful and filled with love. I celebrate the magnificence of living life abundantly.

I call forth a sharer, one who is my equal, who will grow as I grow, that we may grow together. So be it.

Protection

I am protected.

My shield is the love of the Universe. Nothing harmful can penetrate its barrier.

I am safe. God's arms wrap me in protection.

Guidance

I am now guided.

Divine Intelligence is my partner in every area of my life, and it guides my choices and decisions.

My Higher Power is guiding me down the pathway to abundant life.

God is aligning my will with His will.

My steps are divinely guided, as I trust my intuition.

Happiness

I am happy.

I celebrate life with joy and wonder because I am a child of the Universe.

Joy is my rightful inheritance! May I experience its fullness and share that joy with others.

I anticipate with joy the experiences that come to me today and every day.

As I express gratitude for _____, joy overflows from my heart.

As I anticipate the goodness of the Universe, I am filled with resounding joy!

God's plan for me is joyful. I am free now to release all fear and negativity.

As you reflect on your specific desires, affirmations will solidify your worthiness.

Although you may not receive exactly what you desire, there will be something better. Rejection is God's protection because He wants only the best for you.

Unfortunately, our timing is not always the timing of the Universe. By being patient and knowing that your heart's desires are already met, you can relax and wait for the abundant flow. Just because you don't feel abundant doesn't mean that your desires are not coming to you. It is easy to second-guess these steps. You may actually find that you try to talk yourself out of them because you have not seen immediate results. Hang in there! Get excited! More will be revealed! You deserve it!

Words of Wisdom

"For as he thinketh in his heart, so is he." —Proverbs 23:7

"Suffering is always the effect of wrong thought in some direction." —James Allen

"In the infinity of life, where I am, All is perfect, whole, and complete. I am always Divinely protected and guided. It is safe for me to look within myself. It is safe for me to look into the past. It is safe for me to enlarge my viewpoint of life. I am for more than my personality—past, present, or future. I now choose to rise above my personality problems To recognize the magnificence of my being. I am totally willing to learn to love myself. All is well in my world." —Louise Hay

"She lacks confidence, she craves admiration insatiably. She lives on the reflections of herself in the eyes of others. She does not dare to be herself." —Anaïs Nin

"A complete revolution takes place in your physical and mental being when you've laughed and had some fun." —Catherine Ponder

"Within our dreams and aspirations we find our opportunities." —Sue Atchley Ebaugh

"I want to get you excited about who you are, what you are, what you have, and what can still be for you. I want to inspire you to see that you can go far beyond where you are right now." —Virginia Satir

"Love is an expression and assertion of self-esteem, a response to one's own values in the person of another." —Ayn Rand

"Those who do not know how to weep with their whole hearts don't know how to laugh either." —Golda Meir

"Change occurs when one becomes what she is, not when she tries to become what she is not." —Ruth P. Freedman

"You grow up the day you have the first real laugh at yourself."—Ethel Barrymore

"There is a price which is too great to pay for peace, and that price can be put in one word. One cannot pay the price of self-respect." —Woodrow Wilson

"Human beings, by changing the inner attitudes of their minds, can change the outer aspects of their lives." — William James

"Our very life depends on everything recurring till we answer from within." — Robert Frost

"The battle to keep up appearances unnecessarily, the mask—whatever name you give creeping perfectionism—robs us of our energies." — Robin Worthington

"Follow your dream. Take one step at a time and don't settle for less, just continue to climb." – Amanda Bradley

"From early infancy onward we all incorporate into our lives the message we receive concerning our self-worth, or lack of self-worth, and this sense of value is to be found beneath our actions and feelings as a tangled network of self-perception." —Christina Baldwin

"One receives only that which is given. The game of life is a game of boomerangs. Our thoughts, deeds and words return to us sooner or later with astounding accuracy." —Florence Scovel Shinn

"The Universe is run exactly on the lines of a cafeteria. Unless you claim—mentally—what you want, you may sit and wait forever." —Emmet Fox

"A tragic mistake that is often made is to assume that the will of God is bound to be something very dull and uninviting, if not positively unpleasant … The truth is that the will of God for us always means greater freedom, greater self-expression, newer and brighter experience, wider opportunity for service to others—life more abundant." —Emmet Fox

"How I relate to my inner self influences my relationships with all others. My satisfaction with myself and my satisfaction with other people are directly proportional." —Sue Atchley Ebaugh

"The journey of a thousand miles begins with a single step." —Lao-tzu

"Your vision will become clear only when you can look into your own heart." —Carl Jung

"The past has flown away,
The coming month and year do not exist;
Ours only is the present's tiny point." —Mahmud Shabistari

"If a man carries his own lantern, he need not fear darkness." —Hasidic saying

"In the midst of winter, I finally learned that there was in me an invincible summer." —Albert Camus

"Fear is only an illusion. It is the illusion that creates the feeling of separateness—the false sense of isolation that exists only in your imagination." —Jeraldine Saunders

"She had trouble defining herself independently of her husband, tried to talk to him about it, but he said nonsense, he had no trouble defining her at all." —Cynthia Propper Seton

"As I walk, As I walk,
The Universe is walking with me." —From the Navajo rain dance ceremony

For here we are not afraid to follow truth wherever[…]"

"Years may wrinkle the skin, but to give up enthusiasm wrinkles the soul." —Samuel Ullman

"I look in the mirror through the eyes of the child that was me." —Judy Collins

"We have seen too much defeatism, too much pessimism, too much of a negative approach. The answer is simple: if you want something very badly, you can achieve it. It may take patience, very hard work, a real struggle, and a long time, but it can be done … faith is a prerequisite of any undertaking." —Margo Jones

"If we do not change our direction, we are likely to end up where we are headed." —Chinese proverb

"This above all: to thine own self be true." —William Shakespeare

"We should have much peace if we would not busy ourselves with the sayings and doings of others." —Thomas à Kempis

"There is a guidance for each of us, and by lowly listening we shall hear the right word ... Place yourself in the middle of the stream of power and wisdom which flows into your life. Then, without effort, you are impelled to truth and to perfect contentment." —Ralph Waldo Emerson

"To love oneself is the beginning of a lifelong romance." —Oscar Wilde

"Years may wrinkle the skin, but to give up enthusiasm wrinkles the soul." —Samuel Ullman

"Do what you can, with what you have, where you are." —Theodore Roosevelt

"It is the chiefest point of happiness that a man is willing to be what he is." —Desiderius Erasmus

"We are what we repeatedly do. Excellence, then, is not an act, but a habit." —Aristotle

"Let one therefore keep the mind pure, for what a man thinks that he becomes ..." —The Upanishads

"My imperfections and failures are as much a blessing from God as my successes and my talents, and I lay them both at His feet." —Mahatma Gandhi

"The ultimate lesson all of us have to learn is unconditional love, which includes not only others but ourselves as well." —Elisabeth Kübler-Ross

"If one advances confidently in the direction of his dreams, and endeavors to live the life which he has imagined, he will meet with a success unexpected in common hours." —Henry David Thoreau

"Sometimes it is necessary to reteach a thing its loveliness ... until it flowers again from within ..." —Galway Kinnell

"It is difficult to make a man miserable while he feels worthy of himself and claims kindred to the great God who made him." —Abraham Lincoln

"The intellect has little to do on the road to discovery. There comes a leap in consciousness, call it intuition or what you will, the solution comes to you and you don't know how or why." —Albert Einstein

"The past is but the beginning of a beginning ..." —H. G. Wells

"You get to the point where your demons, which are terrifying, get smaller and smaller and you get bigger and bigger."
—August Wilson

"Life holds so much—so much to be so happy about always. Most people ask for happiness on conditions. Happiness can be felt only if you don't set conditions." —Arthur Rubinstein

"If a man happens to find himself, he has a mansion which he can inhabit with dignity all the days of his life."
—James A. Michener

"Anything forced into manifestation through personal will is always 'ill got' and has 'ever bad success.'" —Florence Scovel Shinn

"Tears are like rain. They loosen up our soil so we can grow in different directions." —Virginia Casey

"Desire and longing are the whips of God." —Anna Wickham

"There is a Divine plan of good at work in my life.
I will let go and let it unfold." —Ruth P. Freedman

"I exist as I am—that is enough;
If no other in the world be aware, I sit content;
And if each and all be aware, I sit content." —Walt Whitman

"Be not afraid of growing slowly.
Be afraid only of standing still." —Chinese proverb

"Change your thoughts and you change your world."
—Norman Vincent Peale

"Each indecision brings its own delays and days are lost lamenting over lost days.... What you can do or think you can do, begin it. For boldness has magic, power, and genius in it." —Johann Wolfgang von Goethe

"Be still and know that I am with you." —English prayer

"He that respects himself is safe from others; he wears a coat of mail that none can pierce."
—Henry Wadsworth Longfellow

"Resolve to be thyself; and know, that he who finds himself, loses his misery." —Matthew Arnold

"And the world cannot be discovered by a journey of miles ... but only by a spiritual journey ... by which we arrive at the ground at our feet, and learn to be at home." —Wendell Berry

For those who were raised in a religious environment, the following biblical scriptures can be useful as you come to believe that you deserve abundance:

"Ask, and it shall be given you; seek, and ye shall find; knock, and it shall be opened unto you."— Matthew 7:7

"The eternal God is thy refuge, and underneath are the everlasting arms …" —Deuteronomy 33:27

"According to your faith be it unto you." —Matthew 9:29

"For with God all things are possible." —Mark 10:27

"For God giveth to a man that is good in his sight wisdom, and knowledge, and joy …" —Ecclesiastes 2:26

"Not rendering evil for evil, or railing for railing; but contrariwise blessing; knowing that ye are thereunto called, that ye should inherit a blessing." —1 Peter 3:9

"If ye then, being evil, know how to give good gifts unto your children, how much more shall your Father which is in heaven give good things to them that ask him?" —Matthew 7:11

"So God created man in his own image, in the image of God created he him …" —Genesis 1:27

"But my God shall supply all your need according to his riches in glory by Christ Jesus." —Philippians 4:19

"Cast thy burden upon the Lord, and he shall sustain thee …" —Psalm 55:22

"The Lord is able to give thee much more than this." —2 Chronicles 25:9

"For I am the Lord that healeth thee." —Exodus 15:26

"If ye shall ask any thing in my name, I will do it." —John 14:14

"I am come that they might have life, and that they might have it more abundantly." —John 10:10

"Let not your heart be troubled, neither let it be afraid." —John 14:27

"For my yoke is easy, and my burden is light." —Matthew 11:30

"Behold, I make all things new." —Revelation 21:5

"For this God is our God for ever and ever:
he will be our guide even unto death." —Psalm 48:14

"Ho, everyone that thirsteth, come ye to the waters, and he that hath no money; come ye, buy, and eat …" —Isaiah 55:1

"And this commandment have we from him, That he who loveth God love his brother also." —1 John 4:21

"Finally, brethren, whatsoever things are true, whatsoever things are honest, whatsoever things are just, whatsoever things are pure, whatsoever things are lovely, whatsoever things are of good report; if there be any virtue, and if there be any praise, think on these things." —Philippians 4:8

"Pray to thy Father which is in secret; and thy Father which seeth in secret shall reward thee openly. —Matthew 6:6

"Wherefore, if God so clothe the grass of the field ... shall he not much more clothe you, O ye of little faith?" —Matthew 6:30

"Take therefore no thought for the morrow: for the morrow shall take thought for the things of itself." —Matthew 6:34

"For the word of God is quick and powerful ..." —Hebrews 4:12

"And let us not be weary in well doing:
for in due season we shall reap, if we faint not." —Galatians 6:9

"Delight thyself also in the Lord: and he shall give thee the desires of thine heart." —Psalm 37:4

"And being fully persuaded that, what he had promised, he was able also to perform." —Romans 4:21

"And all of you are children of the most High."—Psalm 82:6

"God is love; and he that dwelleth in love dwelleth in God, and God in him." —1 John 4:16

Recommended Reading

I want to express a great deal of gratitude for the following books and highly recommend them to my readers.

Abundance

Beattie, Melody. *Choices*. San Francisco: HarperSanFrancisco, 2002.

———. *The Lessons of Love*. San Francisco: HarperSanFrancisco, 1994.

Beck, Charlotte Joko. *Everyday Zen*. San Francisco: Harper & Row, 1989.

Byrne, Rhonda. *The Secret*. Hillsboro, OR: Beyond Words Publishing, 2006.

The Dalai Lama and Howard C. Cutler. *The Art of Happiness*. New York: Riverhead Books, 1998.

Dyer, Wayne W. *Manifest Your Destiny*. New York: HarperCollins, 1997.

———. *Your Sacred Self.* New York: HarperCollins, 1995.

Fox, Emmet. *Alter Your Life*. San Francisco: HarperSanFrancisco, 1994.

———. *Diagrams for Living*. San Francisco: HarperSanFrancisco, 1993.

———. *The Sermon on the Mount.* San Francisco: Harper & Row, 1989.

Gattuso, Joan M. *A Course in Love.* San Francisco: HarperSanFrancisco, 1996.

Kasl, Charlotte. *If the Buddha Dated.* New York: Penguin/ Arkana, 1999.

———. *If the Buddha Married.* New York: Penguin Compass, 2001.

Losier, Michael, J. *Law of Attraction.* New York: Wellness Central, 2007.

Ponder, Catherine. *Dare to Prosper.* Marina del Rey, CA: DeVorss, 1983.

———. *The Dynamic Laws of Prosperity.* Englewood Cliffs, NJ: Prentice-Hall, 1962.

———. *The Prosperity Secret of the Ages*. Englewood Cliffs, NJ: Prentice-Hall, 1964.

Real, Terrence. *How Can I Get Through to You?* NewYork: Scribner, 2002.

Real, Terrance. *The New Rules of Marriage.* New York: Ballantine Books, 2007.

Ruiz, Miguel. *The Mastery of Love.* San Rafael, CA: Amber-Allen Publishing, 1999.

Shinn, Florence Scovel. *The Collected Writings of Florence Scovel Shinn.* Radford, VA: Wilder Publications, 2008.

Williamson, Marianne. *A Return to Love.* New York: HarperCollins, 1992.

———. *Enchanted Love.* New York: Simon & Schuster, 1999.

Healing the Wounded Child

Adams, Kenneth M. *Silently Seduced.* Deerfield Beach, FL: Health Communications, 1991.

Beattie, Melody. *Codependent No More.* Center City, MN: Hazelden, 1987.

Bradshaw, John. *Healing the Shame that Binds You.* Deerfield Beach, FL.; Health Communications, 2005.

Downs, Alan. *The Velvet Rage: Overcoming the Pain of Growing Up Gay in a Straight Man's World.* Cambridge, MA: De Capo Lifelong, 2005.

Forward, Susan. *Toxic Parents.* New York: Bantam Books, 1989.

Gil, Eliana. *Outgrowing the Pain* . San Francisco: Launch Press, 1983.

Hay, Louise. *You Can Heal Your Life.* Santa Monica, CA: Hay House, 1987.

Herman, Judith, MD. *Trauma and Recovery.* New York: BasicBooks, 1997.

Jeffers, Susan, MD. *Feel the Fear and Do It Anyway.* New York: Fawcett Columbine Books.

Katherine, Anne. *Boundaries: Where You End and I Begin.* New York: Fireside, 1993.

Lerner, Harriet, PhD. *The Dance of Anger*. New York: Harper & Row, 1989

Mellody, Pia, Andrea Wells Miller, and J. Keith Miller. *Facing Codependence.* San Francisco: Perennial Library, 1989.

———. *Facing Love Addiction.* New York: HarperSanFrancisco, 1992.

Mellody, Pia and Lawrence S. Freundlich. *The Intimacy Factor.* San Francisco: HarperSanFrancisco, 2003.

Miller, Alice. *The Drama of the Gifted Child.* New York: Basic Books, 1997.

Real, Terrence. *I Don't Want to Talk About It.* New York: Fireside, 1998.

Wortitz, Janet Geringer. *Adult Children of Alcoholics.* Pompano Beach, FL: Health Communications, 1987.

———. *Struggle for Intimacy.* Pompano Beach, FL: Health Communications, 1985.

Spirituality

Allen, James. *As a Man Thinketh.* Thomas Y. Crowell, 1913.

Barks, Coleman, trans. *The Essential Rumi.* San Francisco: Harper, 1995.

The Bible.

Chopra, Deepak. *Buddha.* New York: HarperSanFrancisco, 2007.

———. *The Seven Spiritual Laws of Success.* San Rafael, CA: Amber-Allen Publishing, 1994.

Kurtz, Ernest, and Katherine Ketcham. *The Spirituality of Imperfection.* New York: Bantam Books, 1992.

Frankl, Viktor E. *A Man's Search for Meaning.* New York: Pocket Books, 1985.

Foundation for Inner Peace. *A Course in Miracles: Combined Volume.* Glen Elen, CA: Foundation for Inner Peace, 1992.

Hagen, Steve. *Buddhism Plain and Simple.* New York: Broadway Books, 1999.

Kornfield, Jack. *A Path with Heart.* New York: Bantam Books, 1993.

Merton, Thomas. *Thoughts in Solitude.* New York: Noonday Press.

Nouwen, Henri J.M. *Life of the Beloved.* New York: Crossroad Publishing, 1992.

Peck, M. Scott, M.D. *The Road Less Traveled.* New York: Simon and Schuster, 1978.

Prince, Joseph. *Destined to Reign Devotional.* Tulsa, OK: Harrison House, 2008.

Smedes, Lewis B. *Shame and Grace.* San Francisco: Harper San Francisco. 1993

Tolle, Eckhart. *A New Earth: Awakening to Your Life's Purpose.* New York: Dutton/Penguin Group, 2005.

————. *The Power of Now.* Novato, CA: New World Library, 1999.

Torkington, David. *The Hermit.* New York: Alba House, 1977.

————. *The Mystic.* New York: Alba House, 1995.

————. *The Prophet.* New York: Alba House, 1987.

Trungpa, Chögyam. *Meditation in Action.* Boston: Shambhala Publications, 1991.

Watts, Alan W. *The Wisdom of Insecurity.* New York: Pantheon, 1951"

About the Author

J anice Sterling Gaunt, LPC, graduated with a bachelor's
degree from Texas Tech University and a master of arts degree from Amberton University. She has trained extensively
with Terrence Real, founder of the Relational Life Institute,
and Pia Mellody, senior clinical advisor for The Meadows.
Janice is a licensed professional counselor, specializing in

helping both individuals and couples experience abundant living as they overcome the effects of their own childhood trauma.

Along with Tova Sido, Janice has an iTunes top-rated podcast called *The Remedy with Tova and Janice*. She is available for private sessions, public speaking, and workshops. Janice lives with her husband in Dallas.

In addition to *Prince Charming Is Dead...or in Rehab!—A Guide to Dating in the Real World*, Janice is the author of *The Shame Game—Leaving Shame to Live in Abundance*.